WOMEN'S COMEDIC MONOLOGUES THAT ARE ACTUALLY FUNNY

WOMEN'S COMEDIC MONOLOGUES THAT ARE ACTUALLY FUNNY

Edited by

ALISHA GADDIS

APPLAUSE
THEATRE & CINEMA BOOKS
An Imprint of Hal Leonard Corporation

Published in 2014 by Applause Theatre & Cinema Books
An Imprint of Hal Leonard Corporation
7777 West Bluemound Road
Milwaukee, WI 53213

Trade Book Division Editorial Offices
33 Plymouth St., Montclair, NJ 07042

Printed in the United States of America

Book design by UB Communications

Library of Congress Cataloging-in-Publication Data

Women's comedic monologues that are actually funny / edited by Alisha Gaddis.
    pages cm
  ISBN 978-1-4803-6042-6 (paperback)
1. Monologues. 2. Acting. I. Gaddis, Alisha, editor of compilation.
  PN2080.W66 2014
  808.82'45—dc23
                              2014012032

www.applausebooks.com

Contents

Introduction

We all know how it goes, because we have been there.

You have an audition. One where you are supposed to be funny. Really funny. They want you to actually make them laugh…in an audition. And you want to be funny, so funny you book the job, land the part, steal the show!

But you have to have a comedic monologue, and if you see another person do that tuna fish one, one more time, you may gouge your eyes out!

And we don't want that. You need your eyes to see the standing ovation that you will get once you snag the job that one of these monologues helps you land.

This book was conceived because I know a lot of funny people. People who make a living off of being funny. They have performed these pieces and I laughed at them. A lot. A lot a lot. Or they wrote these pieces and I laughed when I read them. A lot. A lot a lot.

It's time to share the love and hilarity.

Book that job. Steal the show. Make them laugh.

And for goodness' sake, don't do a monologue that isn't *actually* funny ever again.

Alisha Gaddis

Subpar Panties

Alisha Gaddis

*Originally written and performed as
part of the show* The Search
for Something Grand.

My manfriend called me on the way home the other day, and said he had a surprise for me. I love a good surprise!

So I said to him,

"What is it?! What!?! What did you get me??"
"It's good!"
"Ooh ooh! Tell me!"
"I did your laundry."
"You did my what?"
"Your laundry. I did your laundry."
"I can't hear you. You are breaking up. I am losing connection…!"

[*Beat.*]

He did my *laundry*.

We are still in the matching, sexy bra-and-undies stage of our relationship. I had—in that laundry the panties you have in the back, back, back, BACK of the drawer. The ones that are beige and see-through from so many washes, with the elastic band hanging out. That used to say "Wednesday" but now only say "ednesda," because the W and the Y have worn off!

This is a full-blown lady emergency!

I rush off to Target to buy new lacy undies. I purchase them and immediately shove them in my bag and head home.

When I arrive home, there is my wonderfully nice boyfriend who has cooked chilaquiles—which I didn't even know what that meant. I had to Google the dish. Turns out it is tortilla chips, saturated in salsa and fried. Exotic, amazing, and delicious—just like him!

I didn't bring up what happened, because I am a white Midwestern lady and that is how we deal with conflict— like it never even happened.

Then in between scrumptious bites—he says,

"I love you honey."
"Love you too."
"You should really treat yourself better."
"Thanks?"
"Maybe you should buy yourself some new underwear."

[*Pause.*]

I immediately went into all the stages of death:

First, Denial—I have no idea why you are saying this. I have no idea what you are talking about!

Then, Mourning—You don't want to love me! Are you going to love me when I birth your children? You never loved me! Nooooooo!?!

Finally, Anger—Fine. We are through.

He knew he hit a land mine of crazy.

He excused himself to the bathroom, where he conveniently stayed for quite some time.

I rushed into the kitchen and went to the shelf where I save every single plastic bag from Ralph's, the 99¢ Store, even Baby Gap—as if, when the end of the world comes, the only way I am going to survive is by tying those bags to my body and floating to safety—why do I save all those bags!!?!?

They are falling on top of me—I am shoving them back up—I grab one—go to my room and put every pair of subpar undies in the bag (except one pair which I hid in a different drawer because you know I am going to want them later)—and hide the plastic bag of undies under my bed. I then took out the panties from Target and slipped them on.

I then went back out to the dinner table and acted like nothing had happened—because that's what I do best.

Later…during sexy, sexy time…my manfriend noticed my new lingerie and said—"Those are nice. Are those new undies?"

To which I swung around and said, "You don't even know me!!"

Santa

Jamie Brunton

Max, honey, why don't you sit down? Now you've asked
Mommy a very grown-up question and I think you are big
enough now for an honest, adult answer. Wouldn't you
agree? Then someday, maybe when you are a little older,
you'll appreciate the fact that I didn't talk down to you.

So here's the truth…yes, Max, Santa Claus is real. But not
in the way you may think. You see, Santa Claus was based
on a real historical figure named St. Nicholas who lived a
long time ago. He was a very special man who gave gifts to
children in need, and now, although he is no longer
around, he still lives in our…

Well…he…died, sweetie. He's….dead now. [*Beat.*] But
that was a really, REALLY long time ago—hundreds of
years, in fact, and…

No, no, no, not the reindeers, too! I don't believe they ever
even existed. I mean, YES, they existed, but not as they

apply to the legend of Santa Claus. I'm pretty certain Santa Claus was from current-day Turkey, or something, so I'm not even sure they have reindeer there. [*Beat.*] Would you like to see Turkey on a map?

Honey, I know you are upset, but let's try to be rational about this, okay?! Reindeer are like deer or moose or like weird horses or something. Ugh, forget I just said that!

What I'm trying to say is that they can't even fly! I mean, yes, reindeer can run really fast but only about fifteen miles an hour or something. To reach all those houses, they'd have to run over a million miles an hour. You know how fast that is? And up in the air, that speed would still be impossible; they'd immediately burn up and vaporize into one big fiery... [*Beat.*] I feel like we should start over.

[*Beat.*]

Sweetheart, I love you. And I'm pretty sure I'm not doing this right. Thing is, I know this seems like a really giant deal right now, but I honestly can't even remember when I found out Santa Claus wasn't real, okay? So let's just take a deep breath, start from the beginning and... [*Beat.*] Oh yeah, I was six, I think...

I was six, and... and they... fighting. Oh god. Too. Many. Cookies. Vomiting. What? No. No, I don't believe it. Not him. Stop it! So many lies. Does this mean my braces aren't (gulp) magic braces? Liars! LIARS! So YOUNG! So (sob) young...

[*Long silence.*]

[*Back in present.*]

Too young. You know what? I was just joking.

Citizen's Arrest

Alisha Gaddis

Hey you! Yeah you! Lady in the red Prius! I saw you throw a bag of McDonald's trash out your window on the 405N.

Yes—I followed you approximately two-point-three miles, or so says my odometer. Why did I follow you, you may be asking yourself? I did so because people like you piss me off! YOU PISS ME OFF! You are a contradiction of the worst kind. You arrogantly parade around flaunting your social beliefs in the face of others with your brand-new electronic car, but in the privacy of your own world—you are a litterbug. Trashing our streets with your gluttony, fast food, and ugliness.

And here you are in the parking lot of a Fresh Foods Market with your reusable bags that everyone can see— probably preparing to buy overpriced organic, farm-fresh bullshit when I saw you smoking secretively in your vehicle. You didn't think anyone would see did you! Well, I did!

Smoking! That second-hand smoke that you sent into the Earth's precious atmosphere is probably silently, but violently, killing the toddler in that cart right there!

[*To lady pushing baby in cart.*] YES! Lady with the baby— push your baby far away and quickly. This lady is MURDERER! A MURDERER I SAY!!! Not to be trusted. But you wouldn't know it looking at her fancy canvas sneakers made out of organic cotton, would you— would you!?!

See—this is my civic duty. To warn people about people like you. Walking amongst us, presenting themselves as if they are freaking honorary citizens of the world, but in reality you are the ones who we have to worry about. Not the gangbanging, 7-Eleven robbing, pimps, but you— drinking your name fancy wine and wagging your fingers at other people's wrongs—the same fingers that are dripping with African children's diamonds.

Lady—you are now under citizen's arrest.

And yes, I cannot actually do anything like write you a ticket or throw your murderous self in jail, but I can stalk you quietly in the corners of your conscience. I will be watching you as you are judging others, shaking MY head at YOUR choices.

Just call me the world police. And you have been SERVED!

Maid of Honor

Carla Cackowski

JANE, *in her late twenties/early thirties, sits at a table in a restaurant. She is having brunch with her best friend,* KATE.

A birdcage veil *and* a diamond tiara? Wow. Well, it is your wedding…Oh, don't tell me what your dress looks like! Let me guess! Um…is it white?

[JANE *smiles wide, desperate to move on to the next subject.*]

I know. I'm joking. No, please, tell me all about your wedding dress. I'm listening.

[*She's not.*]

Waiter! [*Embarrassed.*] So sorry to yell at you like that! My apologies. I didn't mean to be rude, it's just that I *just* realized—the lobster salad I ordered—I don't eat meat! Silly me! It's kind of a new thing and muscle memory hasn't kicked in yet.

[*To* KATE.]

I know what you're thinking, "A vegetarian? What are we, in college?" Right?

[*To* WAITER.]

I'll just take a plain ol' house salad. I know, boooring! Oh! And a glass of Merlot.

[*To* KATE.]

Here's the thing—Merlot is making a comeback!

Ah, yes, of course, back to your wedding. Hey, don't apologize! It's the topic of the day!

(*This is hard.*)

Yay!

[WAITER *drops off glass of Merlot.*]

Mmm. Thank you. Thank you mer-lot. [*Pronounced like "a-lot."*]

[JANE *awkwardly laughs as the waiter walks away.*]

Hmm? Sure, Kate. Yes, of course. You can ask me anything.

[JANE *chugs her wine. She knows what's coming.*]

Your maid of honor? Really? Wow, that's so...so very nice of you! Generous and kind and all sorts of...[*Searching.*] adjectives. But here's the thing, Kate. The thing is... I...well...I can't be your maid of honor. Because. Well... Kate...I could die soon. No, it's not cancer. Not yet! I mean, here's the thing. Who knows how each of us will die, right? I *could* die of cancer. And, man, I would feel real bad if I was your maid of honor and I kicked the bucket just before your wedding, you know?

[JANE *digs deeper.*]

I could also be killed. Kate! Oh my god, Kate! I could fall off the side of a mountain! I do a lot of hiking! I could be mauled by a mountain lion, and in the tussle I could totally fall off the side of the mountain, because you know me, Kate—you know I'd never let a mountain lion take me down without a fight! And then think how much that would suck if your maid of honor fell off a cliff and then you had nobody to count on when you got married? That would suck all kinds of sucky-suck.

[JANE *knows this isn't working.*]

Okay, fine! Kate, I don't want to be your maid of honor!
I'm sorry, but it's too much! I'd have to spend hundreds of
dollars on a dress YOU pick out for me in a color that
YOU like—and let's be honest, Kate, no matter how much
I say I dig it, I will NEVER wear that shit again. I won't be
able to enjoy myself at the wedding because I'll be running
around making sure your drunk mother doesn't hit on the
DJ, making sure the DJ doesn't play the Electric Slide,
making sure that when the DJ ignores me and *does* play the
Electric Slide your drunk mother *doesn't* slip and break a
hip! I'll drop tons of cash that I don't have on a bridal
shower and bachelorette weekend—two parties where you
decide the guest list! And to be honest Kate, I'm the only
friend you have that I actually like! The cake for the
bachelorette party, Kate, I can't be the one to put in the
order for the penis cake. [*Desperate.*] Please, please don't
make me in charge of buying your penis cake!

[JANE *is suddenly ashamed of her outburst.*]

Kate. I'm so sorry. I've just been a maid of honor four
times already, and my credit score can't take another blow
this year.

[*Beat.*]

You will? [*Relief.*] Yes, I'm sure your sister will be perfect! Kate. You're a good friend. Thank you...that's so nice of you to understand...especially since you were my maid of honor last year.

Pageant

Kevin Garbee

Yes, this is going to hurt a little. That's what happens when you get gum in your hair. Stop crying. Stop crying. Young lady…stop crying or I will give you a reason to cry. Now, be still. Fifteen minutes before the pageant. Unbelievable. What have I always told you? "Never eat gum, candy, or sticky things…especially nougat…on pageant day." I spend all this time and money, and you go and do something like this. Keep your head still. Do you ever think about all the girls who would like to be in your shoes? Not to mention the boys who aren't even allowed to be in pageants. Will you stop crying? You are four years old…act like it. I know I would've loved to do pageants when I was your age, but my mother had to work. Keep your head still. I'm not telling you again. So I think you need to take this a bit more seriously and realize the opportunity you have been given. Pageants teach you the importance of looking your best when you leave the house…they help you build confidence…and you may

even make friends from diverse ethnic backgrounds...
which looks very good on a college application. There, I
think I got it all. Now let's run through your dance routine.
And remember, it starts off tap tap shuffle, tap tap shuffle.
Got it? I don't want a repeat of last time... forgetting your
routine... looked like a deer in headlights up there. It was
embarrassing. You should never embarrass Mommy in
front of pageant people. What is that in your hand? Is that
more candy? Don't even think about it. Put it down, missy.
Put it down! All right. Fine. It'll go straight to your thighs.
They'll call you Little Miss Thick Thighs. Is that what you
want? Then put it down. I'll make you a deal. If you don't
mess up your dance routine, I'll let you start eating bread
again. And if you win, maybe Daddy will come home.

Becoming My Father

Jenny Yang

KELLY *is an A-Type Asian American professional who has been seeing a therapist to figure out why she is still having such bad luck with men, especially since she's passed the 30th-birthday mark.* KELLY *is talkative and easily skirts the real issues by talking around her problems.*

Drinking milk makes me fart.

Not smelly deep from the intestines kind. Just a release of pressure, like the column of air that pushes you as you walk into a store with automatic doors.

I can just feel myself becoming my father. He is like a hundred years old! No really. If you round up. Okay. He's eighty-three. He was fifty when I was born! Clearly, I was an accident. And now I have the great distinction of being raised by a father who's older than that blowhole in

Yellowstone. It's so true how when you get old you end up regressing into childhood. Benjamin Button, so true.

My dad farts in public supernonchalantly. Like he's walking down a cold aisle of the 99 Ranch Supermarket with the tofu and just lets it rip. [*Makes fart noises.*] No flinching. No sideways glances to see if anyone is looking. No biggie...Oh that, smell? Must be the fish balls!

I think as we grow into adulthood our subconscious has this built-in alarm system for checking if we are turning into our parents. Heaven forbid we actually learned a thing or two from the people who raised us.

I'm finding myself blowing my nose on a piece of Kleenex...and the actual Kleenex brand, not like some generic store brand that I happen to call "Kleenex." I believe in being precise with what I call things. [*Aggravated.*] The way we say we'll "Xerox" a document, even though none of us are actually using a machine built by the Xerox Corporation. Horrible.

For instance, if your name is Anthony and most people call you Tony but you say you don't mind either way whether we call you Tony or Anthony...I'm gonna call you Anthony. I am willing to give up my breath for an additional syllable if I get to call you what you exactly are.

If you are an organization that has Asian Pacific Americans in your name, then I will always refer to your organization's work as serving the "Asian PACIFIC American" community. Most people forget "Pacific" like it's not the great ocean that touches all of our homelands, you know? We threw them in there for a reason. It would be a shame to make them feel any more left out than they already are.

Don't even get me started on acronyms. What happened to us in the '90s that said it was okay to abbreviate EVERYTHING? I personally blame Calvin Klein and Marky Mark. They made those nuthuggers all famous, hopping onto the coattails of Good Vibrations...and created CK ONE! A [*Air quotes.*] "UNISEX fragrance." I could not turn my head around at school without someone marking their goddamn CK ONE territory, like they are such suburban royalty with their thirty dollar Robinson's May purchase spraying themselves on the blacktop for recess supremacy.

At least before the '90s when we decided to create acronyms, we cared that they made sense. Like the first letters of a string of words actually sounded like something. Like RADAR. Did you know it was an acronym? Stood for "radio detection and ranging." LASER? "Light Amplification by Stimulated Emission of Radiation" Who knew? No one! Why? Because apparently we don't care to know the words behind the word, anymore. Because the word *was* the word!

Now we have ROFL (roh-full)! R-O-F-L! Rolling on the floor laughing. What the hell is ROFL!? Makes no sense. Not laughter. More barf.

Anyway, I'm finding myself blowing my nose into a piece of Kleenex and using the folded up Kleenex to wipe down nearby dust on the coffee table. [*Waits for the therapist's nonresponse.*] Yeah. I know! It totally sounds gross as it comes out of my mouth. But it's not like a ton of snot. You wrap that up and it is STILL good on the outside for a light dusting of the glass table. No streaks.

[*Pause.*]

Oh. Um. What my nightmare means.

[*Thinking.*]

Like, I'm not a "bad girl," you know? But for some reason I was lighting my fart on fire in front of my dad? I've never done that.

Wedding Toast

Laura Mannino

BECKY *stands in front of a wedding reception.*

Hi, everyone. If I could get your attention, please. I'm Becky. I want to mark the occasion of Ann and Jon's union with a few words, and honor my very, very special and dear friend, Ann. As you can tell, I'm not the maid of honor. It looks she's still missing. I wonder where she is. I hope she's okay. I wasn't actually invited, but I wanted to stop by and surprise Ann. Surprise! Ann and I grew up next door to each other. We have so many memories. We spent every single day together. Every. Single. Day. We were joined at the hips. Literally! Remember when I sewed our dresses together and you had no other choice but spend the entire day with me? That was so much fun! Ann and I had a favorite game called "Tea Party Prisoner!" Since Ann was excellent at wiggling out of her clothes and running away, I would tie her up in a chair and we had a tea party for hours and hours with our favorite toys and all of the neighbor's cats and that raccoon. Hey, a little fun fact for you: Did you know that raccoons could commit suicide? Not only did we spend our days together, Ann and I even spent our nights together. We would have sleepovers all the time! I would sit in a tree in front of Ann's bedroom window and watch her sleep like an angel in her bed and then slip away early in the morning before she even knew I was there. Then Ann's parents decided to move away and leave me all alone. Hello, Mr. and Mrs. Johnston. How are you? You broke my little girl heart but I forgive you. Even though Ann's family took her away from me, I managed to still be in Ann's life. Ann might not have seen me in over twenty years, but I've seen Ann! This isn't the first event that Ann forgot to invite me to but I was still there: The piñata birthday party in third grade, the bowling birthday party in sixth grade, the confirmation party at your uncle's restaurant, the high school graduation party in your basement, and then the real party you had with Bobby in the woods behind the school—yeah, I was there at all of them. I took a nine-hour bus ride to every single one of them because that's what real friends do. Real friends never leave each other. Real friends spend their lives together. So Jon, I know you're Ann's husband now, but are you her friend? A *real* friend? If this doesn't work out, Ann, I have a two-bedroom condo down in Gainesville. That second bedroom is yours. Well, I'll have to cut down on some cats, but I would make that sacrifice for you. Well, it looks that maid of honor of yours has returned with some police officers. Well, I'm gonna get a head start. You dance in my dreams, Ann! You dance in my dreams!

White Wine

Kate Ruppert

So, the other night, I had one of my girls over for a drink, and what turned out to be an appetizer spread that reflected all the cultures of the world. I mean, a dream. It was also a hundred million degrees Kelvin outside, and I had chilled a bottle of white wine, because sometimes, you just want a glass or three of really cold white wine on a really hot summer night. This was one of those nights. But you know me, I'd opt for vodka over white wine any day of the week, and it occurred to me that—as we were really getting down to whatever we were talking about and whatever we were chain-smoking over—there wasn't enough chilled Sauvvy B for us both to be using it as a refreshment. So, after the first glass, I posed the question: "Would you rather I be drinking vodka so you can have the white wine to yourself?" And bitch hesitated for a beat, then replied with conviction: "Yeah. Is that too honest?"

Um, what? Is that too honest? Did you just ask me that? Here's the thing: I was hoping that our three-hour, maybe-dramatic gossip sesh would result in the inspiration for a sit-down kinda life-lesson chitty-chat with you, but instead, I was afforded that rarest of rare objective glimpses into one of my own friendships that reassured me that I had found myself a keeper. Can you believe she would ask *me*, "Is that too honest?" Like, okay, look—you know how much I tend to rag on the oftentimes-negative aspects of being a Lady. We aren't nice to ourselves; we aren't nice to one another. We aren't honest with ourselves, and we're not honest with one another. But every now and again, our path is crossed by someone who values the honesty and investment of a friendship over the ease and selfish of superficial. We should all be so lucky to have a girlfriend who is true enough to say that she wants us to switch to hard alcohol so she can keep trucking on the white wine.

I was, honestly, going to reschedule us this week because I was feeling wholly uninspired. But then my wine night happened. I considered not telling you any of this, actually, but then I decided to fuck that, because I'm saying something nice and who wouldn't want to know about that? When you think of saying something kind, you say it; and when you think of doing something kind, you do it. So, here, in front of you and God and everybody, I raise my glass to a dope girlfriend who doesn't beat around the bush, who prefers coming over to going out and who opted to be honest instead of polite. If I've taught you nothing else today, know that bitch, you best strive to surround yourself with Ladies like this, for they will be the only ones who will stop you or support you in decisions which don't come easily. Embrace the gift of being equally matched as a friend and mutually respected as a Lady.

Good story. Now be a peach and get mama another cocktail.

Yogurtplaceorama

Renee Gauthier

I know what you are thinking, and yes, I work out. I work out intensely for about thirty minutes a month. My body is being considered for the next "Bond girl." My face? Oh that just gets asked to audition for plump, quirky roles.

The above has nothing to do with this great observation I had today, other than the fact that I actually worked out. Next to my gym there is a Yogurtplace. Have you seen these things? They are madhouses. Well, I have only ever been to one, and it's a madhouse—so I can imagine the others. I walk in, super exhausted looking, wearing supertight pants, unfortunately.

There is a long line for this self-serve yogurt concept. I line up behind these two very cute, Asian girls. (I say the race of these girls so you can get a full vision of what I went through.) The girls are tiny and cute and for the first minute—didn't speak. Then they unleashed the most "valley girl" talk EVER. I tried not to laugh at first, because it was so weird to hear anyone out of 1987 speak like this— let alone it not come out of a typical trashy white girl.

"He soooooo wanted to tawk to you, last niiiiiiiight. Gaarooosssss." (Gross)

Now, imagine that everything they said down to what the yogurt tasted like was in this tone. After we finally got to the row of fifteen different yogurt flavors, it felt like I was being murdered over and over again. I wanted to tell them, "If I roll my eyes again at your conversation, you are paying for my Lasik eye surgery." (I don't know how much Lasik costs either, but I am sure it is a lot.)

I do want to tell the prettier one of the two that "Jaaaaake doesn't like you if he ignored you all night and then touched your boob when saying good-bye—it means he just liked your boobs."

Christ!!!! Get it together young girls.

I really, honestly almost intervened, but then it was my turn with the sample cups.

Good news about this Yogurtplace trip? ...I got yogurt with strawberries.

The Art of Seduction

Alisha Gaddis

Excerpt from Step Parenting: The Last Four-Letter Word, *as performed at the Comedy Central Stage, 2013.*

In marriage it is important to keep up the occasional illusion of sexy. Yes, I spend most of my weekends in housedresses with no makeup and a slicked-back ponytail, but on the occasion that my partner and I head out for date night—you better believe I am going to shave my legs in the sink and semibrush my hair.

I try to keep the mystique of being a lady alive. Even with a child. ESPECIALLY with a child. But sometimes I fail. The other night, the little one was tucked soundly in bed for the night, and we were lounging on the couch together watching *Modern Marvels*, "The History of Salt"—a show I still pretend to like for the sake of our relationship. My hunk-o-spunk hubby was cuddling into his favorite snuggly sleeping spot—my hipple area—that spot were your waist meets your leg and creates a perfect lady curve. The perfect spot for resting his head. I was supertired and superbored—but casually letting out *ohhs* and *uh-huhs* to feign that I was listening…when I must have slipped into a deep slumber. I was sound asleep.

The next thing I knew—I felt a serious earthquake! I was raised in Indiana, the heartland, where twisters run rampant and earthquakes, on the other hand, are new and scare the living crap out of me. With the urgency of a man on fire, I jumped up and shouted "Earthquake!!!!! Take cover, get in the doorway, get in the bathtub. Go, motivate, move!!!! EARTHQUAKE!!!!"

To which my husband replied, "Baby, baby—that wasn't an earthquake…you farted in my face."

NO! I did not! I am a lady who doesn't toot, especially in my sleep and especially NOT on his face! This could not be!

"Never, I would never! Get in the doorway! We are experiencing a natural disaster!" I shouted.

"Yes. Yes you did." he said calmly. "It was so loud, it woke you up!"

No. No. No. No No! But I am a lady! This could not be. I was in total disbelief! But then…then I felt another one coming. I tried to squeeze my derriere cheeks together and think about a tranquil field of flowers, but come hell or high water—it was coming. I think my husband could see it on my face too, because he said—"Let it out—it is good for you!"

Who says that?! What kind of man says "Let it out!" I farted in his face! If *he* farted in *my* face, I would push him off the couch, demand an apology, and make him rub my feet! Didn't he know I was trying to keep the illusion of seduction alive?

But what had to be done was done.

And he still thinks I am sexy. (But NOT especially sexy at this particular time.)

Cat Lady

Rebekah Tripp

The world is divided into cat lovers and dog lovers. You rarely find an individual so full of rainbows and warm fuzzies that they have the human compassion to love both. Dogs are fine...they're "aight." See, I can say that. I can say, I think dogs are cute. However, have you met a dog lover that can do the same? I challenge you to find one, because all I hear from them is, "cats are the devil," "a cat can't love you like a dog can," "I hate f'in felines." So much angst from the dog lovers of the world!! And yet, I ask you...have you ever seen a cat portrayed in an evil light on film? *Old Yeller*, *Cujo*...the list...is probably longer than two but you get the idea. Sure...the cat in *Pet Semetary* was creepy and evil...'cause it died, was buried, and reborn with an evil soul...you'd be pissy too! Have you ever heard of a fire department coming to the rescue of a dog up a tree? Nope! They leave those dogs up there. There are probably thousands of dead dogs in trees right now because no one cared enough to call to help them out. I believe I've proved my case with these two, valid examples!

No? Not solid fact enough for you? All right FINE! I'll give you some personal examples. Boo, my aforementioned cat, helps me out every day, shows me love in her very own way, and is always there when she deems it necessary—which turns out to be the times I truly need her. In the mornings (I loosely refer to this as morning, because 4:30 a.m. is still nighttime for me), Boo will stand over me as I lie in bed. That b*tch misses me so much that she has to look at me while I sleep. If that weren't enough... she starts to lick my face and even bite me sometimes... just to say... hey... wake up... I miss you. Do dogs do that? Probably not, they probably let their owners sleep all the way through the night, getting an amazing restful sleep ... TYPICAL! Also, a few times, when I've been away for a day or so, and I come home... Boo has puked on my comforter... as if to say, "I was so sick with grief while you were away that it produced a physical reaction." Sweetheart! Dogs probably rarely get sick, and if they do, they probably wait 'til they're outside. Dumb*sses! Last but not least, when I'm holding Boo... like a baby... (Yep, I do it!), there are times when, if we hear a loud noise, she literally attaches herself to me with her claws. She's so afraid that the loud noise might be someone trying to charge in and separate human mother from feline child...that she utilizes her only weapon, her claws, to hang on to me for dear life!! I mean, COME ON!! The evidence is clear here!

So lay off cats and me! I believe that I've presented factoid after factoid giving you insight into the magical world of these domestic angels of love and devotion.

Mom—men love cats!!! And I will find a husband.

But if I don't...I still have my perfect feline life companion.

30

Kate Ruppert

Let's have a quick chat about turning thirty, shall we? I know, the Big 3-0. Oh, wait, no, there is no Big 3-0 slogan for turning thirty. It's just f*cking "thirty." Seriously, really quick chat—it's been one of those weeks where my patience and strength have been tested more times than I can count. I have gone through three whole Xannys (six doses), gone to bed past eleven more than once, regretted plans I've made on two occasions, and (more times than I can count) I have reassured a Lady that she isn't "old." I dunno what it is about the past seven days of my life, but I can promise you that when I recount my stories of woe, they'll all start with "The other day, I felt like I was in the Twilight Zone…" So we're clear, my confirmations of youth have been doled out to Ladies *under* thirty years old. Each and every time. There is something about being twenty-eight and twenty-nine years old that really trips y'all bitches out. And I'd pay top dollar if someone could tell me why.

I know that I have nothing in common with my peers and I feel as if I walked out of the womb a middle-aged woman who no one understands, and I can only conclude that's why the force of turning thirty years old doesn't seem to be hitting me as hard as it has my contemporaries. But I think even above and beyond that, we're presented with an entire generation of women who are somehow resistant to a singular birthday: thirty. What? Seriously, WTF? At what point did we revert to the year 1885, where we declare our worth and accomplishment by how many gentleman callers we've received and how many offspring we've yielded by our thirtieth birthday? I dunno, I feel like maybe it's a bit futile to focus on something that's a foregone conclusion. You're turning thirty. It's gonna happen a few years after your twenty-fifth celebration at Dollar Draft Night, and but a mere blip after your twenty-ninth celebration in Vegas. It's thirty. And if thirty doesn't happen, you can never be present at your child's college graduation. If thirty doesn't happen, you'll never see your child's wedding. If thirty doesn't happen, you'll never know the genius of a fiftieth wedding anniversary. If thirty doesn't happen, you'll never know what it's like to work an honest life and enjoy retirement. You know mama doesn't like to beat around the bush, so why don't you say we get there already? Bring on thirty-one … bring on thirty-three. I think we all want something to look forward to, right? Isn't it strange more of you don't see it that way? What do you think will happen? Like, if you cry about your birthday enough, maybe it won't actually come? It's like going through a pregnancy and thinking you can somehow avoid a delivery. I mean, it's happening. And you know exactly when. Like, *exactly* when. Get over yourself and prepare for it. You have a life to live.

In tenth grade, my English teacher was Mrs. Borchers. She changed my life. (So did Mrs. Segal in eighth grade, also an English teacher. Mrs. Segal had a gavel. F*cking genius.) Both were logical above all else. English is about rules, after all. And there was something about their embrace of logic along with their support of the creative that inspires me to this day, so pretty much anything they ever said to me remains as gospel. At the very beginning of the year, Mrs. Borchers said the following: If you consider college to be the best four years of your life, your life will be a shame. I had known her for twenty minutes, but I trusted she wasn't lying to me. As it happens, I hated high school. I hated college. I hated my twenties. I don't regret anything I did at any point during that time frame, but I hated having to go through it. When I hear a girl lament the loss of her twenties, I have to wonder how it's possible hers were any more enjoyable than mine. Different, I'm certain, but as a twenty-nine-year-old, about to roll into thirty, what in god's name are you going to miss so much? For the life of me, I don't get it.

How many twentysomethings are on your short list to call from prison? How many twentysomethings are on your short list to hook you up with a job? How many twentysomethings would you consider the godparent to your child? How many twentysomethings would you trust investing your money? How many twentysomethings would you consider to be an appropriate representation in a court of law? How may twentysomethings would you ask to borrow money? How many twentysomethings would you want being the example your children are privileged to follow? As a Lady, we aren't taken seriously until we're in our thirties. Sarzy to be the bearer of bad news, but it's true. Hey, how old are you? Oh, I'm twenty-blahblahblahblahblah...No one listens past the prefix twenty. That's just a fact. People assume you don't have things figured out yet. People assume you're a dilettante (look it up; this is a good one to know). People assume you're still in the discovery stage. People assume you still get drunk four to five, maybe seven, nights a week. People assume you're still on your first job. People assume your parents still pay your cell phone bill. Oh, wait, you don't think people assume these things? Then you're straight trippin'. Because where I live, where my parents live, where I grew up, where I moved for college, it's not an assumption—it's a fact. And based on this fact, tell me how remaining in this decade of delusion is still appealing? Get the show on the road already. Forget what you have or have not accomplished. Forget how many kids (or marriages, as the case may be) the people you went to high school with are working on. Forget what your parents are shouting in your ear. Forget about the bar your best friend is setting. Leave it alone. You're you. And you're about to be thirty. Be thrilled. Be thrilled you made it this far unscathed, without an illegitimate child, a Chapter 11 filing, or an "irreconcilable differences" on public record. It's not gonna last forever. Life is gonna sneak on up and smack you in the face, Boo. Like I've said in the past: Eventually, you'll be saddled with more responsibility than you ever cared to have assumed, and there will be no way out of it that doesn't include euthanasia or a prison sentence. Embrace this time you have to continue to learn about who you are. You don't have to shirk your old ways, but you do, most certainly indeed need to learn to burn the Phoenix every few years—your thirtieth is one of the mandatory controlled burns. You can still be you, but sometimes it's best to leave certain versions of you in the dust. Your twenties weren't that great. Be honest with yourself. Why on Earth are you lamenting leaving them behind? There is so much more to life, and the longer you spend slumping onto the stool behind my desk to weep about the loss of your youth, the longer those of us in our thirties are blowing past you. Grow up and move along.

And Happy Birthday.

The "M" Word

Alisha Gaddis

So when you are living together—the inevitable starts happening. Someone starts talking about the "M" word.

Marriage.

Marcus has been talking about the "M" word a lot. A lot a lot. Actually, after two weeks of dating he said to me, "I am going to marry you. You just don't know it yet." Boy's got game. But, now it's been two YEARS!

So marriage, right?! Since you gotta know what you are getting into, I did some investigative Googling on the matter. It seems that so many people go into "till death do us part," but what does that mean? What are the facts? What do I get out of it?

Here are some cold hard facts—

Fifty-two percent of marriages end in divorce??? Fifty-two percent??? If I told you that fifty-two percent of skydiving jumps ended in death, would you do it? If I told you fifty-two percent of trips to the grocery store meant you would hit a grandpa, would you do it? If I told you fifty-two percent of scuba diving underwater adventures ended in self-suffocation—would you do it?

Apparently, we would America.

We are so sadomasochistic, we do it again! Sixty percent of second marriages end in divorce! Third time is definitely not a charm: third marriages—seventy-three percent end in divorce!!

This is from the Census Bureau people! We must really like wedding presents from Crate and Barrel.

But I get it. When I was in middle school—everyone had side ponytails and Guess jeans. Remember Guess jeans? That red triangle on the ass really meant something. It meant that you were somebody. I begged my parents for Guess jeans, but they were too expensive. I left subtle hints, I pleaded, I begged! Finally, they caved. There was a clearance of Guess jeans at Sears. My mom drove me, and picked through the overstock until I found a gleaming pair of white cutoff shorts with sewn fringe and that beautiful red ass triangle. I wore them almost daily. I even did acts so people could see my ass triangle more clearly. Oh, I dropped my pencil—I must bend over so I can pick it up and you can see my red ass triangle! Oh, I carry papers in my back pocket—conveniently placed in the red ass triangle pocket! Oh! It's kriss-kross wear your clothes backward day—I can make you jump jump—BOOM the RED ASS TRIANGLE!

The engagement ring is the modern-day equivalent to Guess jeans. It's too expensive, lavish, and every lady wants one and will do whatever it takes to get it—leave subtle hints, plead, beg!

I never EVER wanted a ring.

Then...I did. I found myself wanting to casually pick up apples at the grocery—reaching out with a giant piece of marked-up glass on my finger so that people would know—I am chosen, I am loved.

My boyfriend must have smelled my weakness. The other day we were doing laundry and he said—hey, let's run some errands while we are out. I said sure. He then pulls up to Tiffany's! TIFFANY'S! I threw a tantrum. Not because I didn't want to be there, but because I had on laundry-day clothes! Sweatpants; messy, semisweaty bun updo; and dirty, nonmanicured fingernails! At Tiffany's! The place with the tiny boxes, and glittery diamonds, and that blue color that people adore. Tiffany's—the place with my possible future ring.

This was a full-blown lady nightmare! I looked like a hobo! I literally dug my heels into the ground and wouldn't move! How horrifying!

So we left...

Do you think I blew it? Oh god. Was that my only chance?!

The "M" word is moving closer and closer—I don't know how long I can hold it off—if I actually do even want to hold it off. Truth be told—I really want that red ass triangle of adulthood—till death do us part.

The Hostess

Laura Mannino

Hi Nancy and Phil! Welcome to our new home! Come on in! John and I are so happy you're here. John! Nancy and Phil are here! Do you want to take their coats? John? He must be in the bedroom dropping off other coats. Well, I'm glad the bedroom is being used for something. Ha-ha-ha, buying, moving, and decorating a new home is just a tiny bit stressful! Ha-ha-ha! I just want you to just relax and make yourself at home. Thank you for bringing wine. How lovely, I can take that…oh, you're putting it on the coffee table. The wine actually goes on the wine table, not to be confused with the beer table, the liquor table, the mixers table, the crudité table and of course the gluten-free table. If you care for any white wine, the whites are on the third shelf on the left side of the wine fridge in the kitchen. Maybe that's where my husband is! John, if you're in the kitchen, can you open a bottle of white? I'd be surprised if he even knows where the kitchen is, because I do everything around here. Ha-ha-ha! Oh! Stacey! Stacey! Hi, there's a coaster right there. Could you be a dear and actually use it? Thank you. Have you seen John? No? Huh. I bet he's in the basement. He's probably now learning to use that power window washer I got him for his birthday that he absolutely hated. He'll do anything including stuff he hates to never be near me! Ha-ha-ha! Oh my god! Okay, no one move! Everyone clear the space. What is that? Who opened a bottle of cocktail sauce over a brand-new rug? Why is there even cocktail sauce? Why is the shrimp ring on the liquor table? The shrimp ring was not scheduled to go out for another thirty minutes and here it is out on the totally wrong table and now there's cocktail sauce all over the rug! John! Okay, everything will be fine. I want all of you to feel at home but I'm sure even at your homes there's clear rules about shrimp rings and their corresponding condiments. Right? I'll just dab this up before it dries. Please stop walking over the stain? Move around me please! Can someone get me club soda? It's in the third cabinet in the kitchen to the right. You'll see it with all the other club soda! The cabinet is labeled "Club Soda." John! Where is John? He probably just stepped out to get some ice or another wife. HA-HA-HA. How is everyone? Can I get anyone a drink? There will be quiche very soon. That is the smell of the quiche burning. Can somebody please take the quiche out of the oven, and get me that club soda, and save my marriage? Is everyone having fun? Hey! Get that fucking bread off the gluten-free table! JOHN!!!!!

Cell Phone

Rebekah Tripp

Recently, I took a trip up to Yosemite. It was freakin'
beauteous!! Gorgeous mountains, beautiful snow...no cell
phone reception! I will admit it, I'm a little addicted to
texting, instant access to my e-mail, a phone call taking a
second to make; access to the outside world in a single
moment. That did not happen in this blanketed "no call"
haven! Oh...it was glorious, folks!! Once back to
civilization, I started to look around me and I became
aware of how truly dependent our society is on our mobile
devices. People connected to this technology as if it were
the umbilical cord of life. Then, I started to further think
on the point and realize that due to our reliance on these
little computers, we have begun to sever our connections
with other human beings.

I have decided to cut the cord, unlike so many people I
come into contact with...

*Chick in my Cardio Barre class who texts and plays on her phone WHILE WE'RE WORKING OUT! Seriously, you're incredibly lucky that the only physical activity that I find I enjoy is this one; otherwise I would throw my two-pound dumbbell at your face. I'm sweating in places that are unbecoming for a lady to mention, and you're sending an e-mail to your fellow shallow pal coordinating your whorish outfits for the evening's festivities. Yeah... I called you a whore... a phone whore. End Call!

*Fellow at my table who sits down while on the phone and remains on the phone for his first fifteen minutes in the restaurant. Well first, dipsh*t, you are probably looking around after five minutes thinking, "Where's my server?" Well Bub, she's right across the restaurant watching your dumb*ss have an epic conversation and is not—I repeat NOT—going to come over to your table until you put the f'ing phone down. I get paid $8 an hour, you're probs going to tip me $4 (I deduce this because...well...look at you). So $8 + $4 = I don't give a sh*t. Don't go into a restaurant until you're off the phone, wait...that sounds... so...simple. End Call!!

*The human being who happens to be on their cell phone at the store while in line at the checkout...face to face...with **another human being**. (I'm sure we've all done this once...don't feel bad...just DON'T DO IT

AGAIN!) Do you think this person loves being ignored? Have you given a thought to the fact that maybe you're being rude? Do you realize that the phone conversation you're having can't possibly be important enough to negate the presence of the person directly in front of you? Let's give these questions some real consideration. The person you're ignoring thinks you're being an *ss, the person in line behind you thinks you're being an *ss, and I KNOW you're being an *ss. End Call!

I think we've all come to realize through my loving and emotionally detached examples that we need to stop the insanity. Honestly, there are a lot of people on this planet... and when all the technology dissolves... you're going to have to interact with them.... So why don't you start now? Believe me, humanity is a significantly better concept than technological globalization.

[*Beat.*]

Wait—hold on a second.... I just have to take this call. It actually is important....

I Never

Alisha Gaddis

I think we are lost. Like really lost. I have no cell phone service. Where in America is there no cell phone service?!? Where, I ask? Nowhere. Only a place that you get really lost in. And we are lost.

How much gas is in the car? Do we have enough to get somewhere? Somewhere that isn't here?

This is the end. We may just die here on this deserted road.

Oh Lord. There are so many things I haven't done! I never took trapeze lessons. I never made my grandmother's noodles. I never climbed Mount Kilimanjaro. I never climbed any mountains for that matter. I don't even have hiking boots. I hate hiking. I never got over my hatred of hiking!

I wanted to start a pyramid scheme. Not one that hurt people and drained their life savings, but one that got me rich—filthy-dirty rich so that I could move to Turks and Caicos and never speak to anyone at my office again! I would just leave my cubicle one day and leave all my pictures up—and my "Happy Hump Day" mug—all just perfectly on my desk. I would just leave it all. They would all wonder where I had gone. They would first be concerned, then scared, then terrified. They would hold a meeting and alert the authorities and O'Connel would say that he wished he had given me that promotion and Marcy would admit she HAD ate my chocolate piece of birthday cake out of the fridge. She knew I knew it all along. They would all cry. They would cry so much! And the whole time I would be sipping some daiquiri with a special name with two tiny paper umbrellas AND a curly straw. And I would be rich—dirty stinking rich. SO rich. And I won't give anyone at the office any of the money. Yes, they are DEFINTIELY left out of my pyramid scheme.

[*Deep exhale.*] I never rode a motorcycle. I never took that cross-continental European road trip, where I planned to meet a man named Alfredo and make love to him on top of his red Vespa. I NEVER OPENED MY OWN VINEYARD!!! I never even stuck my hand in a bag of beans just to feel what that feels like. I have always wanted to try that.

Listen, things are getting more bleak. If we have to turn to cannibalism—I want you to know that I would do it. We should each take a slice out of the other.

[*Pause.*]

No—a pinkie toe has no meat. I will offer my stomach and you—your butt. Best choice.

It isn't going to be easy. But we have to sacrifice for survival.

OH LORD!! I never swam with a dolphin. They always petrified me—I think they can read our minds, but I should have gotten over my fears! I never caught a building on fire just to watch it burn! I never even learned to LOVE!!

[*Beat.*]

Oh my goodness—OH MY GOODNESS!! Thank god! We are saved!—there is a gas station. Saved!

Oh—[*Beat.*] Cannibalism is off the table.

Asian Goggles

Jenny Yang

JANIE *is an opinionated Asian woman (Chinese, to be precise) who is very political and is always questioned about it. She's getting tired of it all.*

I think about race the way some people think about air: it's what I breathe to survive. I don't wake up and think, "Hey! I'm Asian." It's like people in China don't wonder on a Friday night what they're gonna eat and say, "You know. I'm in the mood for some Chinese food." It's just *food*. I'm just a *girl*.

For some reason white people feel the need to remind me that I'm Asian...just in case I forget.

It's my first time at Mammoth, a huge ski resort, and I go to this store to get some gear. I find this clerk, and I'm like, "I'd like to get some snowboarding goggles."

The clerk is a tall, skinny twenty-year-old with long, straight blond hair and a slouchy knit cap, and a long-sleeved shirt under a short-sleeved shirt. She looks at me and says, "Yeah. We got Asian goggles." And walks to the back.

I'm like, "Asian goggles"?! What are they? Extra slanty? What do they have on them? Hello Kitty? When I put them on do I see the world in anime? Asian goggles.

She brings them out and it turns out they're just regular snowboarding goggles with extra foam padding under the nose. Yeah! I'm like, "Oh crap. I thought you were racist! Turns out you're just trying to tell me I have a flat face." "Thank you," [*Looks at clerk's name tag.*] "...Skyler. I'll take them."

They fit great. Oakleys. "Asian Fit." Solid product. Very happy with my purchase.

Technically Single

Kate Ruppert

I guess, based on thirty-some-odd years of being technically single, I have had time to think about some things that most people don't have the time, or perception of reality, to think about. I dunno, things like: Would I be okay just adopting if I never get married? Or: How the fuck am I supposed to share a house with a boyfriend, let alone a husband, or, like, kids and ugly, primary-colored toys?...Sometimes: I wonder if I can knock out a wall in my bathroom and put in a washer/dryer without my landlord knowing...since I'll be living here a while...? You know what I mean?...I think about these things.

But, after a day of reality wedding TV, I also think: Why on EARTH would I have a wedding? I only know, like, twenty people; I cannot imagine wanting to *plan*—or pay for—a wedding; I've no interest in dancing with my dad while people watch us...seriously, there is nothing about a wedding, starring me, that I find appealing. Except the

food and flowers, but that's why Kettle One invented
parties, which is neither here nor there. What I'm trying to
say is that I don't see myself in any sort of personal
wedding environment. Not to say that I don't like them, I
just never thought that I'd be so intimately participating in
one until I told one of my best friends that I am an
ordained minister, and I could perform her ceremony if she
wanted; I'm cheap, easy, and I'd be there anyway. I was
dead serious, but kinda kidding, mostly because I NEVER
thought she'd say yes.

And she didn't say "yes"—she said "hell yes."

Couple of things: I don't go out socially, really, so I don't
generally have cause to dress up. But, I love a good dress.
I'm secure with myself physically, and completely aware
that it's not like my body is going to get better, so I
embrace the shit out of an occasion to wear a dope dress
with full confidence—and, we all know, if you're not
confident, it doesn't matter how good you look in whatever
kind of dress you're wearing. Also, I'm insanely charming,
which means I can go a little more over-the-top with my
gear (over-the-top can err towards slutty, if you're
charming). Anyway, I found a dress; a sick dress. I knew
before I even looked in the mirror that it was going to be
fly. I knew it. But then I looked in the mirror, and I had to
make a heartbreaking determination: I couldn't look like

that at someone else's wedding, because to a bride, her wedding is the most remarkable day and I didn't need to have anything to do with presenting myself as "*that* girl who wore *that* dress." There is not one Institution in the WORLD that I respect more than the Institution of Marriage. None. There's not a single Institution that should garner more respect than that of promising, in front of God and everybody, that you will be honest and faithful and good and respectful and true and fully there. No one said we gotta promise shit to one another, but once you do, you show the fuck up. And I've always said: It's all voluntary, but as soon as you volunteer, it becomes fucking mandatory. And, in this case, it wasn't just that I show up for Aleida in the way that was the most supportive and appropriate (translated: Not wearing that dress), but it was Aleida and James promising to show up for one another, and that shit is for real and forever.

Since we became friends, I have harped on one thing: Mean it. Good or bad, just mean it. If you aren't ready to follow through and show up and go the distance, then— nothing personal—but back up, step away, take a breather. At some point in life, you'll need to quit fucking around, and from the looks of it, some of us, clearly, get that sooner than others.

So…anyway, I'm sorry, wait, what was your question?

Art

Alisha Gaddis

Setting: A museum.

What do I see when I look at this picture?...Hmmm...
Well, I see a candlestick, and a man, and......the top of a
violin? And a vase. A shattered vase. An angry, shattered
vase....

I mostly see that when I squint and turn my head sideways.
Like this. [*Demonstrates.*] I mean, I know this is called
Angry Man Playing Violin-Shattered Vase but I really SEE
that. I do...when I squint.

[*Pausing, looks around and nervously whispers.*]

Okay fine. I don't see that. I don't see that at all. All I see are
a bunch of gray cubes and something that looks very much
like a wiener. [*Whispers.*] A man's wiener. And heaven's
knows I haven't seen one of those in a while. Since the
divorce, actually. Two years, three months, and thirteen

days ago. Not that I am counting! *(Beat.)* And I am moving on! I am going to get my bachelor's in fine arts. I am! This time I don't have a surprise bun in the oven and a future husband who believes that woman should be maternal and stay home with the children while the men go make the big bulk of bacon. None of that bullshit is going to stop me this time! I am a woman of the world—or at least I am going to be! My kids are in college and my husband—scratch that…EX-husband—is off banging his ad-exec partner probably somewhere in the Bahamas—a place he promised he would take me, but did he?!?! NO! He never did!

And what I am supposed to do?! I fulfilled my end of the bargain. I raised our kids. I must say—they are pretty outstanding, the youngest is a little bit like his father, but I think in a manageable way. I kept the house, the finances, did the cooking, cleaning, kid activity management, hosting, smiling, laughing, entertaining, listening—I did it all. I ran that house and our business. And now what…I will tell you!!!

This is my time! My time dammit! I am going to take these stupid art-appreciation classes and drink prosecco in the courtyard! I am going to wear those wedge sandals that he never liked, but I bought anyway and hid under the bed for fourteen years! I am going to go out with my girlfriends and not feel guilty about ordering the steak! I am going to take pottery, and maybe even learn to salsa with a man who has more chest hair than my ex-husband had on his head! I am a wild, succulent woman, and he did ME a favor by cheating on me and our sacred union after twenty-five years. TWENTY-FIVE YEARS!! What an asshole!

But here I am—at this museum, looking at stuff I always wanted to see and never did and actually see now, but don't really understand. But I am here and doing it and no one can stop me.

Oh—don't tell Professor Bliss what I said about the painting. I actually really love it. It made me feel…angry—like that shattered vase. I actually think I really get it. Hmmmm…I think I will see if they have it as a magnet in the gift shop. Ooh! Decadent!

Clowning Around

Tanner Efinger

[*Waving offstage.*]

And a Slap-Hap-Happy-Hoodeldy-Doodledy Birthday to you, Bethany! Eight years old never looked so good. Buh-bye! Bye bye now!

[*She sees a sad kid waiting on the curb.*]

Hey! I recognize you. You were the "Sad Sally" at the back. What's wrong? Aren't you going to go home with your friends? Is your mommy gonna pick you up? . . . No? . . . Not much of a talker are you? Well that's fine because I'm off the clock anyway. Here. Hold my nose.

[*She takes off her nose and gives it to the sad kid. She massages her own face.*]

My face cramps up if I wear that thing for too long. Can I be honest with you? I hate this job. I'm just not really a kid person. No offense. What? Don't judge me. I bet you've have your fair share of bottomless and profound ironies in your seven or eight…years of…well, maybe not. I'm sorry. I talk too much. I always have.

[*She sits down next to* SAD SALLY.]

What are you so sad about anyway? Don't you think it's hysterical that I'm wearing a rainbow wig and balloon pants? No? I guess I don't find it that funny either. I mean what possible reason could you have to be sad? I mean look at me! I'm as sad as it gets, but you don't see me frowning. Well, yes, I do have a gigantic smile painted on my face, but you know what I mean. I mean look at me! Seriously. I'm a birthday clown because, hey, it pays the bills. I'm thirty-two and I've never been married, engaged twice but never married because who wants to marry me? Right? I mean who in their right mind would want to marry a birthday clown who hates kids, can't cook, can barely keep a plant alive, and can't even have children herself. See the irony now. Woo hoo! What a catch!

Oh, just ignore me. Over share! Can I have my nose back? Thanks.

[*She puts her nose back on and makes a funny face.* SAD SALLY *laughs.*]

Hey! You laughed! [*They laugh together.*] Thanks. I needed that. I really needed that. You're a really good listener...

Rudolph

Rebekah Tripp

A few friends of mine recently engaged in their favorite, time-honored holiday tradition—gathering in front of the ol' boob tube and watching the fabulous claymation creation, Rudolph and the Misfits. However, they about cried into their spaghetti when they realized that the Rudolph and the Misfits version that they had DVR'd and spent countless days counting down to, was not the one that brought back that flood of holiday spirit. This abomination that they were watching was a redone, re-created, ruined version of the original.

Rudolph, as most…if not all…of you know, was the reindeer that was a little different from the rest. He was taunted and teased, ousted from the normal reindeer activity because he didn't look exactly the same. However, as it turns out, that thing that made him different ended up being the thing that saved the day in the end. Rudolph was special, and recognized as that. Then all those uppity motherf*ckin' reindeer loved him and recognized him as a viable part of reindeer society. (Yes, morally, that is still a little off, but it's better than nothing and hey...they're just reindeer...it's not like humans would do that...Oh, and also...in this claymation version, there's a prospector named Yukon Cornelius and a winged lion named King Moonracer...drugs anyone?) Anyway, apparently this new version of Rudolph fast-forwards into his future. What... might you ask...does he do now? Is he a Habitat for Humanity volunteer, the CEO of a nonprofit corporation who finds jobs for homeless reindeer, the inventor of the energy-saving lightbulb? Nope...he's a f*ckin celebrity. Yep, he goes back to Misfit Island and is loved and lauded and...that's where my friends stopped watching so...I don't really know what else happened. However, what I do know is this—Rudolph is no celebrity. The new version is horsesh*t.

The story of Rudolph the red-nosed reindeer is a life lesson. It's the ugly duckling dressed up for Christmas. If we take the essence of the story away, kids lose the message. We need our children to realize that yes, they are freaks of nature, and yes, eventually someone will love them once they develop an unusual skill or talent that is needed or interesting. I jest (a little). Honestly, though, the message is a good one.

I used to feel that Rudolph was my spirit animal, but now I just feel like a misfit toy.

Nesting

Alisha Gaddis

My boyfriend recently told me that I lacked the domestic gene. The "domestic gene?" I didn't even know that existed. He told me that HE loved nesting, and I didn't like nesting, and most women my age would love to be nesting.

What is nesting?

And women my age?! What?!

Now—I have fought my entire life against the stereotype of the role of woman. What is she supposed to do—cook, clean, carpool? Who is she supposed to be—a wife, a mother, a saint? I have fought hard and rough, not as a feminist, but as an equalist. I know how much less women get paid than men, how many women aren't the heads of Fortune 500s, and how many strippers are single mothers (a lot!). But as soon as I heard that I wasn't domestic—I went apeshit!

Sure—I never think to send thank you notes. Sure—every time I cook I get third-degree burns, and I don't see the need to vacuum—ever. Sure! But not domestic?! How dare he insult my womanhood? Why did this affect me? Why do I feel that I want to have this gene that seems antiquated and against all my core beliefs. Nesting—my ability to bake bread, and tend my home, and raise my unborn children?!?! I can baste a freaking turkey—I just don't want to.

So, I told him that he can build a nest while I build the nest egg—and then birth the babies to nestle in it. BOOM!

Teen Angst

Carla Cackowski

JAX, *sixteen and dressed all in black, stands in front of a microphone. She does her best to be confident, but the pigtails that slip out from underneath her hoodie don't help the tough-girl image.*

My name is Jax. Prepare to laugh, open-mic people. I mean, I can promise nothing, but you should be prepared just in case.

Sometimes my mother looks at me and says, "You're dressed like a serial killer." My response to that is always, [*Creepy voice.*] "Well Mom, I guess that means you're dressed like my next victim."

[JAX *is momentarily nervous. And then, as an aside:*]

(Don't worry. I'm not really a serial killer.)

[JAX *takes a deep breath and gets tough again.*]

My father was Son of Sam…My grandfather's name was Sam…My father never killed anything except for maybe my mother's spirit.

My stepdad always says, "The problem with sixteen-year-olds is that they think they can joke about anything, because they've experienced nothing." My stepdad is forty. The problem with forty-year-olds is that they are fat, balding fuck-tards.

[*JAX turns to someone in the front row and asks:*]

Where are you from?

[JAX *hears the answer.*]

I hate that place.

Sometimes my mom cries that she's afraid she gave birth to an unhappy child. I feel like it could be worse. She could've given birth to a vagina-chomping reptile.

Last week my real dad sat me down at the dining-room table and said that I like to say things just to shock people. Which is so not true…[*Quickly.*] I like to masturbate to Dexter.

[JAX *doesn't hear laughter. She pulls the hood of her sweatshirt down and gets real.*]

What the hell? This is some pretty funny stuff. I don't
know what your problem is—you guys thought that fifty-
year-old dude up here making jokes about his prostate was
hilaaaaarious! I thought he was pretty boring. He didn't
even ask for my phone number.

[*Beat.*]

Oh, I guess that red light means my time is up. Hey,
Lighting Guy, I guess this finger means—

[*Just as she's about to flip her middle finger,* JAX *realizes*—]

Oh. Um...Can someone give me a ride home?

And Then There's Europe

Danielle Ozymandias

YAM, *on an airplane, is nervous. She checks her seatbelt, her watch, and finally, to the passenger next to her, she says:*

Hey there. Hi. Normally I love to fly, ya know? Wheeee. And I'm not psychic. I'm like, totally unpsychic... nonpsychic? But, my whole family is in touch with the ethereal plane. I have an uncle who helped solve a murder! Me? Normally, I don't even know if I've let the cat out— oh, god. So, if I have a dream that I'm gonna die, I have to wonder. I mean, since I've never had a "premonition," doesn't one predicting my death seem, at the very least, appropriate? See—I had this dream two days ago that we crash. So I wrote farewell letters. I told everyone how much I love them, and I apologized to Mom for—well, the teen years. And I left very specific instructions on how to handle my remains 'cause I don't want them screwing that up, and then, because in the dream we don't burst into

flames or anything—we just crash into the ocean—I put
everything in a watertight baggie and I put it in my bra.
[*Pats her bra.*] Who finds luggage? Nobody finds luggage.
Bodies they recover. I really thought this out. And then I
got on the plane…and I've been sitting here, for five hours
and the stewardess keeps asking if I want peanuts…[*To
stewardess.*] No, thanks. I'm waiting to die. [*To passenger.*]
Maybe I should get a drink—what goes well with death?

Ya know, dying on a plane has got to be the worst way to
go. Think about it. Your last meal is airplane food. Your
last movie? If, you didn't already see it before, it's probably
because you didn't want to, and now, it's twenty feet away
on a four-inch screen with bad audio and the five-year-old
behind you keeps kicking your seat!

[*Pause.*] And nothing. I mean, not even turbulence, which
is at least exciting if you're in the bathroom. Frankly, I'm
disappointed. I'm like the complete opposite of psychic—
if I think it's going to happen, it definitely won't. [*Pause,
brightening.*] Well, at least that's predictable!

Christmas in Chicago

Renee Gauthier

This holiday season started off with a standby flight to Chicago, Midway Airport from LAX. Flying standby is totally new to me, and I lucked out by getting on my planned flight. I was in line to board and standing next to a gentleman that most Midwest folk would consider "typical."

Balding, chubby guy in his thirties just making witty banter to cover up any insecurity he may have, not realizing that I have the same ones. Seems nice enough chatting up myself and a lucky girl behind us in line. This guy was lucky enough to be sandwiched in line by two magnificent ladies. He knew it. Everything seemed fine as we inched up the line until he started trying to slowly go ahead of me! Ya know when people do this? They inch up a little more until they are next to you threatening a position takeover?

I make a face that proves that I will not go down easily, as I am carrying my three-legged dog in her travel bag, and this guy doesn't know that I will not only unleash my b*tch, but I will release my dog's b*tch as well if he tries any funny business. We are close to the actual plane entrance, and I hear in a soft tone.

"Motherf*cker stupid b*tch son of a f*cker."

I realize this is coming out of my chubby, line-cutter friend. I try to not make eye contact in fear that if he knows that I know he is swearing, he might get nasty. I then keep hearing:

"Motherf*cker, f*ckin stupid f*cks."

I then have the revelation that this guy has real-life Tourette's. It's real!

I act natural as he zones in on me and starts with:

"So where you heading to?"

I respond with "Chicago."

He looks at me and says, "Yeah, but where are you heading to?" In a tone that says, you don't live in real Chicago. I respond with "Chicago," and he aims the same question to the poor girl behind me.

Finally, he looks at me and says, "I'm going to Wheeling, you know you probably don't know anyone there other than your church pastor."

I say "Not even then" not realizing my now chubby, line-cutting, Tourette's-having friend is a full-on Christian.

He spends the rest of our line time talking about Christ (with the random swearword rant shoved in). Then, as he is trying to advance in front of me as we are about to step on the plane, I "accidentally" hit him with my "dog-in-a-bag."

I look at him and apologize—as I am actually carrying my dog in this bag.

He then says "Oh! There is a dog in there? I am carrying a dead body."

I kind of laugh, but realize that he might not be kidding. This guy bumps into my butt more times than normal as we find seats, and I am happy to say he was forced to sit somewhere far away from me. I can only imagine what that poor mother of two small kids had to endure on that flight.

Manners

Kate Ruppert

Every night, I go for a DP. Stands for Dope Powerwalk. Pun intended. I travel at a very rapid rate of speed, and I look *ridiculous*. Which is why I get stoned. I'm too self-conscious to look like that and be aware of it. Anyway, the path is about four-and-a-half feet wide. One person goes one way, one person goes the other. Period. Not two people go one way if they have two in their party, and the other person moves off the path. Not one person goes one way as does their dog on a leash, and the other person moves off the path and still gets tangled in the damn leash. And certainly not two men go one way and refuse to step out of the way of the Lady coming the other way, forcing her off the path into a tree. That is definitely not how the etiquette of a two-way path goes. Further, not stepping aside so a Lady can pass is a hideous violation of any sort of manners you were raised with no matter what the rules and regulations of the park may be.

Manners.

That's where I'm going with this. Here's why I'm going there: Someone has to. For the past almost-four years, I've been an office manager for a big company that does things that I don't know about. Not because it's shady, but because I don't have time to be interested in our business. I'm far too busy doing the dishes, making the coffee, listening to problems and/or joyous news, receiving feedback on the weather and how we may be able to change it going forward. I spend my days hearing about how the fifteen dollar car wash at work "isn't competitive with the one down the street from my house"; I'm swamped with the worry over the temperature of a coworker's cubicle, or the way the light hits their computer screen "which makes the third line hard to read sometimes." I could open my own Netflix distribution center with the number of red envelopes that have been left on my desk over the years because my desk is "the same as the mailroom, right?"

Occasionally, I'll get pulled aside so someone can ask me about getting a different kind of green tea in the kitchen, because the fourteen varieties of green tea (which are but a sliver of the $500 a week I spend on tea as a food group) are somehow not adequate; my days are spent buying Airborne tablets—which we go through at a rate of 100 million per minute. (Heads-up morons: It's like a f*cking glass of orange juice, it's not an antibiotic.) Today, I looked into getting fruit salad for a party forty-eight hours from now with color-coordinated fruit—"if possible; sorry for the last minute!" I make sure there are enough Rolos in the candy mix for those who like Rolos, and enough York Peppermint Patties to make Hank think I put them there just for him. And, but not limited to, I've been known to make signs for the Ladies' bathroom stalls that remind said "Ladies" to wipe down the seats they pee on; or I'll whip up a friendly reminder for the Men's room that reads "If it's brown, it must go down." Further, they request these signs be "funny like you do, you know?" Every single day that I show up for work is another day that I am whisked through the world of behavioral psychology. At the very center of it all is the glaring lack of manners.

This is for the guy who didn't say hello to the cashier before giving his coffee order, nor did he thank her when he was done. This is for the girl who only tipped her delivery guy three dollars even though he brought her food at ten p.m. in the driving rain. This is for the man who "helped" the guy at the car wash wipe down his car so he could ensure it'd be done right. This is for the husband who couldn't seem to find the trash can in the kitchen, so he just left the tea bag in the mug—which only made it as far as the sink. And most certainly, this is for the woman who couldn't put down her phone long enough to pay for her groceries. Based on what I've seen transpire at my office on a daily basis, I think I work with every single one of these types. I've experienced a true cross-section of manners and lack thereof, enough to know that y'all need to step it up. Not saying hello to someone you work with as you pass in the hall is not an option. Leaving trash on the floor of the kitchen because you assume it's within someone's job description to clean it is lazy. Deciding to talk on your phone instead of to the real person standing in front of you is not appropriate. Thinking that complaining can be masked as constructive criticism is a falsehood. And assuming that there could be any circumstance which would allow for omitting "please" and/ or "thank you" is obscene.

We're all in this together. We all have good days and bad days. We all have f*cking bullshit shit in our lives that would drive a weaker man to drink. But when it comes down to it, unless you're dead, you're doing okay. If you're working in my office, driving your dumbf*ck Prius or in line behind me at Starbucks, you're doing okay. There is no reason in the world to be an asshole. None. Unless there's a reason, then okay. But, honestly, that doesn't happen too often. And when you roll on around like you can be an asshole just because that's gonna be your "thing," then not only did it backfire—because now you're just an asshole and your "thing" is that you "used to be a nice guy who thought it was funny to be an asshole"—but you've also turned into a rudy. There are few more deplorable qualities in a person than being rude. So gross. But y'all are rude. Let's check it. Let's understand that while that B*tch may have cut you off in traffic, she's still a Lady B*tch, so giving her the bird is crass and wholly inappropriate. Let's remember that while the barista definitely screwed up your order, it's his one hundred jillionth order of the hour, and all one hundred jillion people in front of you have decided that "Asshole" would be their new schtick, too, so, maybe he *does* have an attitude, but maybe it's a good time to be mature and not unleash on the kid and allow it to derail your day. Let's appreciate the 15 Items Or Less line when you actually only have fifteen items or less, and not when you have…Or 20-to-21-ish-Items-If-You're-In-A-Hurry.

Don't ever underestimate the power of manners and doing right by your fellow man. You're going to spend the rest of your life benefitting from or paying for how you treat people. It's in your best interest to act accordingly. I don't believe in karma, but if I did, I'd say karma is a b*tch. I actually do say that all of the time. It's true. That shit will f*ck you up. I've seen it happen. I've *had* it happen. I'd start leaving 20 percent and doing your own dishes.

And I most certainly would NOT force ME off MY path during my DP anymore, lady—just mind your f*cking manners!

New Phone

Alisha Gaddis

Entire conversation takes place on the phone to her mother.

Mom? Hi! I can hardly hear you. [*Beat.*] I am on
speakerphone? [*Beat.*] Okay—no problem. You got a new
iPhone! That is wonderful news! How fancy! Moving into
the technological age! Now you will be able to FaceTime
with all your grandkids. [*Beat.*] FaceTime?...That is where
you talk on the phone but see each other's faces. [*Beat.*] Yes,
it is like Skyping. But it isn't Skyping—it is FaceTime.
[*Beat.*] I don't know why they don't call it that. It must be a
different company. But yes—it is the same.

You can't see the buttons? Well, just turn the phone
longways. Like sideways, and the buttons will get bigger.
[*Beat.*] I don't know how. [*Beat.*] Yes—like an iPad. Well, it
is the same company, that is why. Mom—why are you
laughing hysterically? [*Beat.*] You think that is genius? It is,
actually. [*Beat.*] Okay—I won't tell Dad that I told you

about this. Why, though? [*Beat.*] Let me get this straight—you want to act like you figured it out all your own so you look like a genius? Okay. That makes perfect sense. Gosh, Trevor is so much like you. [*Beat.*] He is! My brother is like you, and I am like Dad. I mean that in the best way. I am saying that because I gave Trevor the idea of getting Michelle a baby present. A push present to be exact. [*Small beat.*] A PUSH present. For pushing a baby out of her vagina. [*Beat.*] Mom—I can say *vagina*—I am a 32-year-old adult and that is its name. *Vagina*. [*Beat.*] Yes, I am in public, Mom. I live in Los Angeles. People say a lot worse things than *vagina* here.

Anyway, I helped Trevor with the idea for a push present—he didn't even know what it was either, and I sent him tons of ideas and stuff, and he took my idea and got her a present and she LOVED it—he didn't even tell her I helped. Which is fine. I don't need credit. Really, but I just see where he gets it now. [*Beat.*] Yes—I am talking about you. He gets it from you! [*Beat.*] I am not shouting at you, Mom! I am just saying.

Okay, anyway. What did they tell you at the phone shop? [*Beat.*] It didn't come with instructions? [*Beat.*] Okay. Just Google those on your iPad and use the iPad while you work on the iPhone. They want you to hook it up to your home "The Wi-Fi." Just say "Wi-Fi," Mom. Not "The

Wi-Fi." Like "Facebook," not "The Facebook." [*Beat.*] Yes,
Mom—I did write that on my Facebook. Why?! Because I
think it. [*Beat.*] I don't care if Aunt Clara gets mad about
my stance on gay marriage! I think that everyone deserves
to love who they want—that's a human right! She had a
crappy marriage and is divorced three times over already.
Doesn't she think other people deserve that same
opportunity to be happy then unhappy then happy then
unhappy again? [*Beat.*] She can call me a bleeding-heart
liberal if she wants—I take it as a compliment! What is
wrong with having a heart that bleeds with care and love?!
Nothing. Absolutely nothing. I don't care if she doesn't
want my name in the Christmas drawing. She can put my
name back in the sock! I am not even coming home this
year for Christmas! [*Beat.*] I already told you that, Mom—
don't get upset. Don't cry! Mom—I have lots of things to
do for the holidays here—I just can't—and the plane tickets
are so expensive—and the snow! Okay, okay, okay—I will
come! Just stop crying, okay?! . . . Geez.

What, Mom? [*Beat.*] Dad is there now. Okay. He wants me
to know that he doesn't want "The Apps." It is just "Apps."
Not "The Apps" . . . never mind. Okay—then he doesn't
have to put Apps on his phone. You have to put them on
your actual phone. [*Beat.*] How? If you don't want them,
you don't need to know.

Celine Dion? Yes—she can be your ringtone, Mom. [*Beat.*]
I do. I do think that is a good choice—for you. [*Beat.*]
What is my ringtone? ... The theme song for *Sex and the
City*. Yes, Mom—I did say "sex." MOM!!

Okay then—if I am no help at all, call Trevor. [*Aside.*] (He
always helps you anyway.)

Oh—you already called him? ... [*Beat.*] His line was busy.
Fine.

Okay, Mom. I love you, too. Call me tonight on your new
fancy phone.

[*Beat.*] Yes. We can use The FaceTime.

Death by Zumba

Moreen Littrell

A few weeks ago, I was having a GREAT day. I was drinking a smoothie, the SUN was out, my MOONROOF was down. I was listening to "SUSSSUDDIOOOO" on the radio. And then I got a voicemail from a distant relative who I don't talk to that much—my mom—saying, "I'm afraid I have some bad news. Call me."

Do you believe that? Motherfucker. I. JUST. GOT. A. SMOOTHIE. !!!

So yeah, *Mom*, I'll get right on it. I'll just turn down "Sussudio," finish my text, take the next exit, and call you back so I can hurry up and get your bad news. 'Cause you know they never just leave the bad news in the message. No, if its bad news, they want you to GUESS.

[*Calmer.*] No, I GET why people don't leave the bad news on the voicemail. I mean you can't just blurt out: "Dad's dead. Call me back." 'Cause that would be insensitive. Unless of course your dad was an asshole. Plus there's the potential for misunderstandings. "I thought you said Grandma got run over by a reindeer?" "No I said Grandma got hungover drinking root beer. With reindeer."

But the problem with NOT saying WHAT the bad news is, is that the bad news could be ANYTHING. And involve ANYONE. And your imagination can run wild with all the possibilities. Like the bad news could be . . . my . . . sister. She could have been abducted by pirates. Or it could be . . . my . . . sister . . . and she could have been swallowed by a shark. Point being, you get your hopes up.

[*Sad.*] But my sister was fine. She called me and told me the bad news: Grandma died. And I was like, "Oh, why couldn't it have been YOU?!" which apparently I said out loud so I had to say, "It's not that I WANT you to die—it's just that if it's between you and Grandma, I would have preferred it to be you."

And then she told me that Grandma died doing . . . Zumba.

I was like, "Oh my god, Grandma did drugs??" She was like "No, it's a dance. Like Jazzercise." She then told me I had to call the rest of the family and tell them the bad news.

Okay. But first, I'm going to YouTube to look up this Zumba thing. And I found out that Zumba has this move that Jazzercise totally does not have. It's called the BOOTY CIRCLE. (Perform the "booty circle," a swiveling of the hips with isolated torso…) And THIS is how my grandma died.

So then I called the rest of my family. But if I got voicemail, I wasn't going to make them guess, so I just left the message that Grandma died doing Zumba. A few hours later my cousin calls back and says, "Grandma died doing Roomba? Vacuumming?" "No," I said. "Grandma died doing Zumba." Another cousin calls and says, "GRANDMA DIED doing the booty circle?" "No," I said. "Complications related to the booty circle."

The upside to my grandma dying is that I got to go home to Oregon and see my family…minus one. And we got to do things together that we haven't been able to do as a family before…like bury Grandma. And my family all came to an agreement that tap dancers should perform at the end of her service. Unfortunately, we forgot to ask what music they were going to dance to. Because when it came time for the finale, the showstopper, the tap dancers came out, past my grandma's coffin, tapping to "We're in the Money." Although a classic, I don't think that's on the Top 100 of best songs to tap-dance to at a funeral service.

At the end of the service, a woman came up to me and asked, "So, what did she die of?" And I said "Zumba." And the woman said, "Well at least she died doing what she loved." And I said, "In fact, she told me right before she died that the thing she loved more than anything was the 'booty circle.'"

Crushed

Alisha Gaddis

We just moved in together! We live TOGETHER. I know! I moved in with him. He just moved into a new house that I had to okay, because he said that he picked it with me in mind. That's huge. Do you think I still have rights?! Why do I need rights?! What rights do I even need? Why am I already worried? Oh my. I moved in with a man.

Don't tell my mother. If she finds out I am living in sin— that is a whole other bag of worms.

We moved in together this past week, and I immediately had my first minor meltdown—where I am going to put my shoes? We can't combine our shoes!! Mine are too fragile! I am too fragile. His giant boots could crush my pointy-toe polka dot pumps! He could crush my heart! His Converses smell like man sweat! Can he smell my fear? Was moving in together a mistake?!...Moving in together WAS a mistake! What have I done!!!

[*Beat.*]

But he reassured me that this was not a mistake—that everything has a solution. This has a solution.

His solution—we build shelves. Shelves will hold my shoes and my things and my life. A shelf can be just mine, even in the land of together.

To get those shelves—we had to go to Ikea. People love Ikea. They say oh—you can get dressers, wine glasses, and Swedish meatballs all at the same place.

I hate Ikea.

I am very afraid of the Swedish. They are big and confusing and blonde. Every single time I go to Ikea—I end up in a bunk bed—in the fetal position, crying. I am not even lying to you. I have a panic attack. Every time. All the aisles, and you don't really know where you are, and you can't get out, and they have small pencils, and then they send you on a scavenger hunt to a giant room with large boxes that are labeled in a different language where nobody works in. Suspicious. The Swedes.

Well—we went to Ikea.

And I didn't cry—for the first time ever. I DID break into hives, and he bought me a Swedish ice cream.

I think that's symbolic.

We got home, to our home, and then we had to build what we bought. And it is all in pieces and the directions are in Swedish and no matter what you buy—they tell you that you only need one tool—this tiny metal L. What is that? That is a trick! Damn you Ikea. Damn you Swedes.

But I am onto them—Ikea furniture building tests your relationship from the very beginning. If you can't build a foreign coffee table with a microtool—how can you build a successful relationship? Is that in the instructions, IKEA?? Is it?!?!

But my boyfriend and I—we build shit. We built the shit out of that shelf. We built it and now it lives in our home. Housing our shoes. Mine have plenty of space. They don't feel crushed. And neither do I.

Eggs

Rebekah Tripp

Easter eggs equal colorful and beautiful and then yummy once you crack them open and eat the contents. Deviled eggs equal the best use of a chicken's egg ever…EVER! Over-medium eggs equal amazing on a burger…if you haven't tried this, do yourself a freakin' favor. Robin's eggs equal interesting when you're a kid and you find one on the ground and you don't know what to do with it so you take it home and hope that if you love it enough and keep it warm it will still grow and hatch into a baby robin that you can name Pierre Fernando Larry Bird that will always love you and be your pal…just me? Oocytes equal a mature egg released from a female's ovaries. My oocyte equals MY business.

I will tell you why I bring this up. Lately, my oocytes (let us just call them "eggs" since oocytes make me think of something out of a biology book, and appropriately so)…okay, so my *eggs* and what I choose to do with them seem to be the topic of conversation lately. Everybody thinks its super fun to ask me when I'm thinking of having kids. (Granted, I realize that it takes more than just my eggs to make a baby; however, that sh*t is the main ingredient.) Yeah, I'm married…to the luckiest man on Earth. Yeah, it's been five years, which is longer than some prison sentences. Yeah, I do eventually want to spawn another human being. This is my issue, though: Why does everyone think this is an appropriate question to ask, say, on a regular, normal, no-babies-around Tuesday? You'd think I'd be ready for the question, since people started asking me ON MY WEDDING DAY…but it always catches me off guard.

Now you know two things about me and the topic of children. One, you'd be more surprised if I called you and told you I was pregs than if I called and told you I was in jail. This is because my dose of what they call "the maternal instinct" is real tiny. I'm about as maternal as the average man is romantic. Second, I do think kids are fun…to mess with. You can basically tell them anything, and they will believe you. I use this to my advantage and I overuse this to my amusement.

Regardless of whether or not I should actually be allowed to have a child…which I should…eventually, this is not a topic of conversation unless we've at least watched one episode of *Sex and the City* together. Yep, that's how close we have to be. It's like an acquaintance or stranger coming up to a preggers and touching her belly (by the way, when I am pregs, that sh*t will not be tolerated)—it's off-limits to you. So, chat with me about the weather. Chat with me about how much you like my new haircut. The topic of my procreation, however, is off the table folks. Thanks.

But I am really happy for Tricia. She is going to be a great mother, and you threw her a lovely shower. And that diaper tree—freaking amazing.

Cavemen

Alisha Gaddis

Do you think there were gay cavemen? I mean really, do you?

Is that an okay thing to even say?

What I mean by that is—was sexuality even an issue when
they were freezing in loincloths being chased by wooly
mammoths all whilst trying to perfect the art of fire? I
mean—did anyone really think about who was putting what
into where and what went with what and how? Was Susie
cavewoman emotionally attached to Stefano the caveman,
or was he the only one closest in age who had all his
fingers? Did Susie care if Stefano was getting play from
Frank the group leader? Did Frank and Stefano share a love
of brontosauruses and a lust for each other? What were the
moral implications of the Neanderthal community? Were
there ethical codes? I mean—if we really get down to the
nitty-gritty—did people even know who they were related
to? Did they even care??!?! Were Susie and Stefano first

cousins or—worse—brother and sister? Or brother and brother? Does it all really matter? They are all dead and we don't even know them! They could have loved each other and the T. rex's (sexually) for all we know!

But I bet somewhere along the way—someone was hurt. Love, back then, was real too, right? Someone, somewhere, in some dark cave, drew some hieroglyphic of her unrequited love to a certain someone. Somehow, somewhere—someone was hurt. Love didn't just appear one day. When human life was thrust onto the planet, love was born as well.

Love and loss and regret and pain are just facts of life. Horrid, bitter, stupid facts of life. And it can happen to anyone—anywhere.

[Beat.]

I bring this up because I think Paul is gay.

[Beat.]

Shit. It even sounds worse when I say it aloud. I have never actually said it aloud. Only whispered it in the shower. I think I did that though because I was hoping he would hear...He didn't. He was singing Celine Dion too loudly whilst watching Rachel Ray...

We have been married thirteen years, you know. Very happy. Very social. Very active in the community.

But I know he is gay. Gay gay gay gay. I have always known. Deep down. I knew as soon as he complimented my pleated skorts and knew which season my Polo Sport turtleneck was from. But that didn't stop me from loving him and him loving me. And we LOVE each other. But he loves men. The man form. The man parts. I know it. I see him. I see him look and look away. One time, four years ago, we even shared an awkward laugh because we both caught each other staring at the same hunk of spunk at the pool in Palm Springs. And I have been keeping him from that. So, who am I to judge after all these years? Only his wife.

I may look like a fool. Like a desperate, stupid fool, but I am going to tell him I know. Tell him to go find his Stefano and be the saber-toothed tiger of his soul.

I need to release him from the confines of hetero and thrust him into the world of gay. GAY GAY GAY GAY!!!

[Beat.]

Just as long as he still cuts and colors my hair biweekly.

Audition

Kevin Garbee

Hi. My name is Amanda Flynn. I'm managed by William Abrams United Creative Artists Talent Group. I don't have an agent yet...so if you know of any good ones...wink wink. Anyway, here is my headshot and résumé. And I just want to thank you so much for this opportunity. This is my very first audition. I have been waiting so long for a break like this. I mean, I've been out here for months now. And I just want to say that I can do any role...I'm ready for this...I belong in this room...I love eating healthy and taking care of my body...and I deserve to be happy. Sorry, my acting teacher would have killed me if I didn't do my affirmations. Maybe you know him. Bob Picot? He's awesome. So talented. He did like two episodes of *The Ropers* and a *B. J. and the Bear*. It was really kismet that we met. I was having a really hard time figuring out, you know, which technique would be best to make me a star, and then I ran into Bob...literally. He lives in my building...and I was texting one of my girlfriends...not looking where I

was going...and I literally bumped into him at the
mailboxes. Turns out he teaches acting...it's called The
Picot Method...and it combines Adler and Chekhov and
Hagen and Stanislavski and...is it pronounced Meese-ner
or Mize-ner? Anyway, it was perfect for me. He calls it
Alexander Technique for the Mind. And it's been life-
changing...life-giving actually...because his method is
really all about breathing. And he does this thing...you
know how a lot of teachers tell you to be in the moment...
to act moment-to-moment? Well, Bob's thing...he calls it
Verisimilitudes...is to act moment to the moment
following the next moment. So you actually skip a moment,
which allows the audience to not anticipate what's going to
happen. It has so made me a better actor. And then his
Inner Voices Technique...it blew me away. You see, Bob is
a very spiritual person...as am I...which is why I
immediately connected with him on so many different
levels. So he has this Inner Voices Technique, which helps
you tap into your past lives to play roles more truthfully. It
gives you so much to pull from. I mean, I can play Dirty
Harry just as easily as I can Little Orphan Annie. And I
cannot break character for, like, days...I mean, I can't pee
like a man...but other than that, I am the character. So I'm
going to do a monologue from *Hamlet* because, according
to my psychic healer, I was a real prince in a past life. And
if you can, just imagine that I'm in a cemetery.

Investment Piece

Alisha Gaddis

No, this seat is not taken, but I really need to leave my purse on it. See, I can't put my purse on the floor, because this is an investment piece. I read this article in *Chic Chick* that said you need to invest in your wardrobe and the woman you want to become—who you see yourself as in the future.

The article had a top ten list of things all women most certainly need if they are ever going to be anything in this life. The list included a little black dress, a trench coat, nude heels, a pop of color, a string of pearls, a high-quality bra, a printed umbrella, a classy scarf, a perfect for your skin-tone lipstick, and an investment piece—a name-brand handbag. As you can see, I have all of these things on. I look amazing. And I better—I am off for a job interview, and since I maxed out all my credit cards to buy this outfit, and this is the fourth job interview I have had this week, and I can only wash this LBD (that's "little black dress" in fancy talk) in the sink so many times—I better get this job!!!

I mean, I am not trying to panic here, but how much more overqualified can I be to get an internship at a bloody marketing firm!!! I went to the best college, I moved to the big city, I even joined a sorority so I could talk about it in interviews—just in case! But oh no, I am mediocre! I am run-of-the-mill! There are a dozen girls with the same degree right on my nude heels trying to trip me, cause me to fall, and then walk on my back into the victory lane of success!!

Doesn't an intern just get coffee and make copies?!? I should be running Manhattan for god's sakes! Did you know I was salutatorian of my high school class? Then, magna cum laude from my college? Played field hockey and swam freestyle relay! We medaled! Every summer instead of hoochie-ing it up in Cancun—I volunteered to teach children to read in Ghana! I donate white blood cells to homeless women, built a well in Central America during a megadrought, and made made-by-hand shoes for little people in China! What more do they want from me!??

I will tell you—they want my nails to be chip-free and my hair Brazilian blown out, and my outfit to look like it is dry-cleaned, even if I can hardly afford ramen noodles or my cell phone bill!! The hypocrisy of it all!

But I am going to take this fancy, clean purse and get off this subway, and go get this job!

And when I get off—you can have both my seats!!!

Until then—go play your ukulele to someone who will give you some change, because the only change I have is a change of heart over my life choices and you don't want a piece of that mister. Trust me! Now back away! This seat is taken!!!

Toast

Danielle Ozymandias

So, I'm at the airport. And, of course I have to go through a security checkpoint. And I'm a little worried because I'm smuggling a small container of nail polish remover in my coat pocket. Well, that stuff is flammable. They don't let you take it on an airplane. And for a two-day trip I haven't checked any luggage. I don't want to take the remover on the plane—I just want to do my nails in the next three hours while I wait. So I walk boldly through and it goes off, and it's my barrettes. I mean, a quarter-sized square of metal has set the damn thing off. So I stand while they run the wand over me and discover that indeed, I am not a crazed lunatic but a well-accessorized individual. And I'm feeling pretty good because they have not discovered my two ounces of liquid acetate. And I stand there and wait for my bag. And I'm waiting and waiting, and it's not coming out of the x-ray machine and the line is backing up behind me and people are flashing me angry postal worker looks and then the conveyor belt starts moving. So I go to grab my bag—but the belt is moving backwards. There are two security guards at the machine, and the younger one takes the bag, flips it over and sends it back in. And I'm thinking, well, I packed pretty tight—they probably can't see everything. And I wait…and I wait…and these two guards are looking at the screen, both of them women, and finally the younger one taps the older one on the shoulder and says, "It's okay, let it go." And I realize that they have just found my hastily packed nine-inch, hand-held, battery-operated, chrome dildo and mistaken it for a bomb. Of course, it could have been worse—instead of just staring at me like I was a sex-crazed lunatic and talking about me in the breakroom, they could have whisked the dildo away to the bomb squad while they interrogated me in a very small, badly lit room where even my accessories would not have made me look good and they would have found the nail polish remover.

Consumerism

Alisha Gaddis

My heart won't stop beating. I cannot believe what I did. Well, actually I didn't really do anything—but I kind of did. A little bit, but not really. Oh my god! I could go to jail!! Can I go to jail? Oh my god!

Okay—here is what happened. You know I love all the clothes at K & L's—I mean who doesn't!?! And I always buy basics from there—if I can. I mean they ARE pricey. Like way too pricey. I mean, you can get almost the exact same thing at Forever Young for literally half of the price, but anyway.

So I went into the dressing room—you can only try on eight things. Which is a lot, but not a lot for me, because I had everything in two sizes. You know how I have been on that juice cleanse? I mean—if I eat one more kale leaf I will vomit, but is super working, but not all-the-way working. I have to keep doing it for another week. I am right in

between a 4 and a 6. Talk about inconvenient. A 4 makes
me look muffin-top-try-hard, and a 6 makes me look
slightly homeless! Talk about stressful! Anyway—I had
about twenty-four items. That's WAY more than eight,
right? So I had to put a few on the door. But you know
how that is—you just reach out and switch what doesn't
work. Swap one for the other. Whatev. And I found this
really CUTE outfit. Adorbs navy sailor-esque blazer,
cotton boy tee, sherbet lacy tank under, and washed-out
neon-green skinny jeans. Can you picture it?! OMG right?!
So CUTE. So I went out paraded in the full length—loved
it. Took it off and went up to buy it. I deserved it.

Bought the outfit (the girl at the cash register was so
cute—she totally loved my new reverse mani), about to
leave the shop, and BOOM the sensors explode! I am
buzzing and beeping and blinging and I am super
embarrassed, but I am like—WHATEV...I have the
receipt. I am like waving the receipt so everyone knows I
didn't steal anything. Like laughing you know? I show the
scary man that is carrying a weird stick baton—not even a
gun, but a stick baton—my receipt, and I try to crack a joke
and he is like Stonewall Jackson or Stone Cold Steve
Austin—whichever one that doesn't smile.

But then he is like, "No Miss, it is your shirt," and I am all
like, "WHAT?!?!" Then I realize...I am wearing the tank!

I left the sherbet tank on! I bought the whole outfit but left on the tank. I forgot to take off the tank! Why would I try to steal the cheapest thing!?!! If I was going to steal something, it would be the blazer—it was sixty-nine ninety-eight! The tank is like twelve dollars. This is absurd!

I wouldn't steal. But then I have been back here and I am like—OMG. Did I steal it? Did I do this on purpose? Is this a scream for attention? Did I feel like if I didn't have this tank that I would die from non-post-consumerism? Nothing has been really exciting me lately—and I felt a huge rush when those bells and whistles went off. Did I want that? Is this who I am really am?!!? Am I going to become a nameless face behind bars swallowed up by the system?!

OMG!! I cannot take a life in jail. Mom—please get me out of here. I promise I will never accidentally on purpose steal again! PLEASE.

[*Breathes a sigh of relief.*] Thanks, Mom.

Mom—is it okay if I borrow your car again tonight—I wanna wear my new outfit to Stacey's birthday party?

Jury Duty

Jamie Brunton

Phew! What a relief. Waiting for your name to be called at jury duty is so nerve wracking; it feels like *The Hunger Games* for ugly people. Present company excluded, of course. Then again, why are we so freaked out about being picked in the first place? At least it would be something new…

I forgot to bring something to read. I'm usually okay with that. I can just stare into space for hours. It drives my parents nuts. I tell them, "I'm not *dazing* out. I'm *stressing* out." I run through every decision I need to make, every outcome. I go over and over what I'm not doing right in my head. It's actually very productive. I've pinpointed exactly all the reasons why I'm not happy.

Do you know when the lunch break is?

Hmm… If my name is selected, I can't decide if I'm going to try and get out of it or not. What are you going to do?

Yeah…I don't know either.

It's just…I don't know if I have the right to pass judgment on anyone. I mean, I live with my parents. I'm dating someone who won't call me his girlfriend and I pretend I'm okay with it. I've shoplifted before too. I stole beer from the grocery store when I was seventeen and then felt so guilty I threw it out on the side of the road. I was driving and just tossed it out of the window. My friends were pissed!

Yeah, I might try to get out of it. I've been looking up excuses on my phone. One man said he had to urinate every fifteen minutes so he couldn't serve. Another woman claimed she couldn't be on a murder trial because she'd been a murder victim herself—can you believe that? [*Beat.*] Stay away from Yahoo! Answers though, they're mostly just calling each other gay.

My aunt got out of jury duty once by faking Tourette's and yelling racial slurs. She's started doing it all the time now. She thinks it's discouraging people from kidnapping her.

Funny, isn't it? We'd rather let a room full of strangers think we're racists than spend a few days sitting around. When, let's face it, that's probably what we'd be doing if we weren't here anyway. There are likely two people here total that actually need to be at their jobs right now. By the way, I never realized how many of my peers were "self-employed." By the looks of them, being your own boss isn't quite the dream we all thought it was.

They are calling names again...

Dammit! [*Then, calling out.*] Here.

Boulder Holder

Alisha Gaddis

You know I can't even remember getting my first bra. Do you think that means I was, or was not, traumatized by the experience?

I DO remember being really young, maybe four or five, and my mom taking me to the department store and having to walk by the lingerie section, and I would get so mortified I would become visibly angry.

Why was I so scared of a few pieces of lace hung together by some elastic and metal clamps? Yes, if I put it that way—it DOES sound a bit medieval, but it is a tool for our lives as ladies.

There is nothing wrong with the fabric that holds our breasts up to the world! Breasts are a beautiful thing! Not only do they attract the male species—for god knows what reason—but they can eventually FEED a baby. Breasts

FEED little persons. They are desirable decors that can produce food! There is nothing that compares to that!

Boobs deserve entire stores, catalogues, and parades just for them—and that is why they have them. We celebrate the tits, the mammary glands, the fun bags! As women—we shout at the top of our lungs—these are my gazongas—they may be big or small or lopsided or dark or thin or saggy or perky or somewhere in between, but they are mine! I am proud of these girls.

Today—I want YOU to feel liberated as we pick out your very first boulder holder! My little girl's buds have sprouted into full-blown flowers. You, my dear, have a blossoming bosom and we shall get you a bra—not only because you need it, but because your breasts—peeking out into the world—deserve it. Ta-dah! Here are your ta-tas!

Honey—come back here and stop crying! Feel the power of your jugs—overflowing with newfound abundance! Power to your peaks!!! I give a hoot about your hooters!

[*Aside to salesperson.*]

(This one in white and beige please.)

The Spice Channel

Jenny Yang

ALICE *is a Korean American 1.5 generation professional. She grew up enmeshed in the Korean American Presbyterian Church community in Torrance, California. After pursuing import car modeling and semiprofessional ballroom dancing in her twenties, she feels rather shaky about her faith. She's confessing this like she did something really bad.*

It was channel 47. At first I didn't know our TV went up that high. I don't know if you remember this, but TVs used to have antennas. And there wasn't always an actual channel for every number. You had to skip. It's kinda like our channel list was missing teeth.

And if you had cable, and didn't pay for like HBO and Showtime, it was "scrambled." The image looked like you could kinda get the channel but you had extremely bad reception. The sound came in and out. You could only make out black and white shapes kinda moving, but kinda dancing around the frame.

Freshman year, my two friends and I went to my house to hang out after fifth period cuz we didn't have volleyball anymore so it was like free time. I lived so close to North High. For good students like us, the closest thing we could do to feel kinda "bad" was get off campus before finishing sixth period [*Beat.*] cause our volleyball coach let us. That's the day my friends and I discovered... The Spice Channel.

My friends and I got home and started snacking on some Choco Pie and kim pap. Perfect afternoon snack. Usually, we can just talk about whatever, but we decided to find something good on TV. My friend Mina had the remote and just started going higher and higher on the channels. I mean, what's there to see? And then she gets to channel 47.

[*Wide eyes.*]

Holy crap. What's that noise?

Mina stops channel surfing.

Moaning. [*Mimics the sex moan, but it's clipped at the end, like dropped TV reception.*]

[*Sex moan, quick little bursts.*]

My other friend Jenny is like, "Oh my god! It's a porno!" [*Aside.*] (She's Chinese... [*Whispers.*] and not Christian.)

Mina just spun her little head around to look at us…wide-eyed…giggling.

She's like, "Oh my god."
I'm like, "Oh my god!"
Jenny's like, "Shut up!"

I go up by Mina, sit down cross-legged and stare. At this point, we can't see much from the moving shapes and static. The sound cut out. The three of us sit there. Cross-legged. Staring.

Mina whispers to me, "I think that's her butt."

Sure enough, we're getting a better picture. We can practically hear all the sounds at this point.

This pale naked lady with long wavy brown hair and thick bangs takes off her robe and gets into this antique tub in the middle of this big room. [*Whispers.*] She's touching herself.

[*Says conspiratorially.*] Then this guy…looks like a biker…comes over…takes his clothes off…damn! We can't see his penis. Too blurry…so he comes over, gets naked and jumps into the bathtub, and grabs her…

SHIT! Static!

Jenny's like, "I think they're humping." We get really quiet.

[*Confessing.*] I'm sitting there, my breath is faster...and I start feeling warm...and tingly...down there.

[*Beat.*] Mina's like, "You guys, this is kinda weird."
[*Fake upbeat.*] Yeah! It's kinda weird! But I look over and Mina's still staring, mouth open.

At some point I realize this couple is on a motorcycle speeding down this open highway. Their hair is whipping in the wind and she's straddled behind him...then she starts rubbing...him. [*Beat.*] In the front. [*Gestures around crotch area.*]

[*Says intensely.*] At this point, I have to shut it down. I'm getting paranoid! Like my parents will walk in on us, even though it's just two-thirty in the afternoon! I'm sweating. I've been crushing this piece of kim pap in my hand for the last five minutes.

"Okay, Mina. Change it. [*Beat.*] Now."

[*Long beat.*]

Ugh! I want the sex.

The Image of Perfection

Alisha Gaddis

Oh god. Oh god. OH GOD!! She will be here in approximately twenty-three minutes. Roger. Roger! ROGER! Did you leave the cones out front so she can park directly in front of the house? I don't want her to have to park down the road like she did last time. That was so mortifying. Stupid street cleaning!

Rose! Rose!! Get in here.

[*Beat.*]

Is your room clean? Don't embarrass mommy. Make sure you put your dolls back on the shelf and make your bed. There is no excuse for messiness this time. You are four now. Time to step it up.

Oh my. I think my migraine is coming back.

Roger. Roger! ROGER!

Honey, did you empty the dishwasher? I felt horrible when she was here last time and those cups were in there. That was just horrific. Oh god.

I am getting dizzy. I cannot take this pressure.

Do I look all right? Should I change? Is this too fancy? Does this say "relaxed and kind," or does it say "professional and loyal"?

Which one?

[*Beat.*]

No—it cannot say both.

WHICH ONE?!?!?

Rose—DO NOT TOUCH THOSE PILLOWS!! I have fluffed them to perfection!

Roger, is that the doorbell? Oh god. Oh god—she is early!

My migraine. Oh god—I can't see.

Okay—breathe and smile everyone.

[*Beat.*]

What?!? Excuse ME, Roger. I do not care if she is our cleaning lady, but I personally do not want to appear like a slob to anyone.

I don't care if she is going to do the job that I have already done. I would be humiliated if she saw our dirty socks and leftovers. I wasn't raised in a barn, you know. I cannot let someone see the gritty underbelly of this family. We are pristine champions. And we will act accordingly.

ROSE—DO NOT TOUCH THOSE PILLOWS!!!

Roger—open the door and let Juanita in. Everyone put on a happy face and DO NOT LEAVE HANDPRINTS ON THE WALL AS WE LEAVE THE HOUSE TO LET HER CLEAN IT!!

[*Beat.*]

Hello Juanita! So good to see you again this week! Sorry our home is such a mess...

Berkeley Liberals

Jenny Yang

DANI *is driving from Los Angeles to Berkeley to watch the University of Oregon/Cal college football game and hang out with old friends. She is driving with her boyfriend, who is listening intently in the passenger seat.*

You see how this guy got out of the fast lane? Common courtesy. NO ONE does that in Berkeley. Some asshole will just be all slow and "duh." You know why? Because no one else matters to them.

After Oregon kicks Cal's ass, we are getting the hell outta Berkeley. I don't even wanna drive within a ten-block radius of Berkeley Bowl. I swear they hold membership meetings for condescending liberals there.

Man, fuck Berkeley! Fuck Berkeley and their "I'm a liberal" self-righteous pedigree!

[*Long beat.*]

Well, I'm "heated" because they suck. We get it. You had the sixties and seventies where you got some shit done. And now, what are you doing? Selling artisanal gelato? Fuck, your artisanal gelato! Mocha Gojiberry Crunch? Kill me with thirty-one flavors of ice cream and shit down my throat before I spend ten dollars on half a scoop of that bullshit. Cuz that'll feel better than getting a whiff of condescending attitude every time I have to trip over your hemp dog leash choking your miniature schnauzer...takin' a shit in front of Berkeley Bowl.

[*Under the breath.*] (Pampered little fuck.)

[*Long beat.*]

I am NOT overreacting.

I grew up with these people. Berkeley is Eugene is Seattle is Portland. But, man, you don't know true White Liberal Asshole until you hang out in Berkeley. They're a special breed of Asshole.

We're gonna meet up with my friend, Joleen. I grew up with her in Eugene. The sweetest kid. Her parents moved them to Berkeley after middle school.

This one time I went down and stayed with Joleen when we were playing Cal. I was minding my own business eating cereal with her when her parents just couldn't resist pulling me into this fucking "workshop" they were having at their house.

So Joleen's parents, Gary and Maxine, are these big-shot child psychologists. Joleen was raised with NO television and NO sounds in the home until college. [*Long beat.*] "Nonviolent parenting." BULL. SHIT. She wasn't supposed to but she watched TV at my house. But like, there were NO SOUNDS. At all. In her home. They even padded all the doors and cabinets in the house! Nothing could slam. Nothing. I swear she had blankets that lined her kitchen cabinets. Shit was not falling hard on anything.

So I'm eating breakfast but it's one big room so I'm pretty much halfway into the living room right behind their little circle. It was a bunch of pregnant mothers learning about "gentle birthing" and creating a "nonviolent home."

Fucking Gary and Maxine started talking about how "our spirit is interconnected with our surroundings" and how "our children are the tuning forks to our existence." Some mumbo jumbo bullshit that sounded like they were making it up as they went along. It was so gross. I mean, you'd think they were starting a cult. These motherfuckers had no boundaries. I mean, they made each pregnant mommy stroke each other's bellies the whole time during this lecture.

So I'm just sitting there, and at some point during this sermon Gary's like…"If I may, Dani, case in point…Dani, come on over here." "If I may"? Like I could say, "no"? I just walked over with all these eyes staring at me.

Gary started to pull at my face and lift my arms, talking about how being raised in the "mainstream" environment had "physical consequences." I was in so much shock that I didn't just walk away immediately. Like, I was confused. Then Maxine started to say all these things like, "Dani's experienced so much chaos as a child. She was constantly expressing her rage when she came over to our house with little Joleen. We just knew she needed more of our influence…" and on and on and on.

Finally I snapped out of it and just walked away. I was just like, "Okay. Okay."

[*Chuckles.*]

I mean, MY parents were fucking naked-ass pot-growing hippies. And I grew up with some shit you would not believe, but that's completely real. Now Gary and Maxine were on some other level shit that made no fucking sense.

You can use touchy-feely words, a Cal degree, and some chanting, but no hippie costume you wear can cover up "Asshole."

Like who grabs a kid...your kid's friend, not even your own kid, and talks shit about them openly like they weren't in the room? This is while they were teaching about "gentle parenting"?

[*Beat.*]

Yeah. Joleen doesn't hang out with Gary and Maxine so much anymore.

Me

Kate Ruppert

I apologize a lot. A lot a lot. And it drives me crazy when other people do it, so it must drive other people crazy when I do it. I tend to speak quickly and definitively, and it can deliver as sarcastic or judgmental. And since I have an obsession with human behavior, I replay conversations I have over and over and try to "figure them out."

I like asking people if what I'm saying makes sense or if they feel like I'm being bossy or patronizing. I want to know how I'm coming across. I like customer feedback. And I genuinely want to know.

I love turning everything into a study of behavioral patterns. I'm obsessed with logic. I love figuring out, deciding, and executing how to get from Point A to Point B—and how you got from A to B. While I do think there is a most efficient way to do something, I don't think there is a universally efficient way to do it. Everyone gets there differently. I just want to know the logic that got you there.

I also like very specific driving routes.

I put my car keys with whatever I need to remember to take. I can't leave without my keys, so I'll never leave without whatever it is I'm supposed to remember.

I take my showers at night before I go to bed because I'm already up, so why not? And it means I get to sleep in. And also, getting into bed clean is a good idea. For all kinds of reasons. And, I can't just go to bed. I have to go to bed and do one last phone Facebook check, or I have to play until I win at Solitaire or Mahjong. And I check my alarm twice-ish to make sure it's set.

My morning routine takes forty-five minutes. I am up at seven, sometimes earlier, never later; I am in the car at seven forty-five—sometimes earlier, never later. I wash my face, then brush my teeth, then put lotion on my face, Vaseline on my lips, mascara on my top lashes only, and perfume behind my knees. In that order, never different, and then I am done with the bathroom portion.

When I leave my house, I stand outside my front door and say, "I locked the door and blew out the candle." I won't remember doing either one of those things, but I will remember telling myself I did and I won't think about it again.

I practice my handwriting. I change letters I've written a certain way for years because I feel there is a prettier way to do it. Sometimes, I want an easier way because the awkwardness of having to write it ruins the flow of what I want to write and how I want it to look. So I practice it over and over until it looks the way I want it to. I just changed my uppercase *G* and *J*. Both are lowercase at all times now because they flow from one letter to the next far easier when you eliminate their right angles.

I like to be reasonable rather than diplomatic.

I never mind asymmetry as long as everything is in proportion. I'm obsessed with proportion.

I hate confrontation, but I like conflict.

[*Pause.*]

I digress...what was I talking about?

Yay!

Alisha Gaddis

My sister is pregnant! YAY!!! I am so excited for her—like
REALLY excited for her. My baby sister is having a baby!
Two years younger than me isn't much. She is only two
years younger. Just two years.

Did I say I am excited for her? Really, really excited. So
excited to be an aunt.

[*Beat.*]

Is it okay not to be really excited? ... I mean, I am thrilled
for her. But I also have this feeling deep in my stomach. I
am not jealous per se—I just feel weird, like I got punched
in my gut really hard. Really, really hard. But happy style.

I mean, she has only been married for a year—but I guess
it makes sense. But, she is two years younger than
me ... Having a baby first.

AND—I am getting married. This year. This is MY year.
So the timing is incredibly convenient—for her.

Is it wrong of me to tell her/ask her/TELL her—not to
announce her pregnancy at my wedding? I mean—she will
be showing, which is totally adorably cute—I just don't
want everyone fawning over her...[*Under the breath.*] (like
always).

I mean, I am so happy for her—so happy. But couldn't she
have waited another five months?!?! She already stole my
thunder by getting married first, especially since she is
younger and I have been dating Mark for longer than she
even knew Rafael! She got a home first, a dog first, and
even got her driver's license in high school first—I cannot
help it I am near-sighted!!! She stole my middle school
boyfriend, my place on the volleyball team, and I know my
grandma likes her more! But a baby first—at my
wedding?!?! ARE YOU KIDDING ME!! WHAT A
BITCH!!! WHY CAN'T SHE JUST LET ME HAVE
MY MOMENT!?!?! MY MOMENT IN THE SUN!!!!

[*Beat.*]

Seriously though, she is going to be a great mom. I am
really excited for her. I am. But I swear to god, if she steals
my future baby's name—I will KILL her!

The Breakup

Rebekah Tripp

Wait…don't say anything. Let me just get this out. This is going to be hard enough without that sweet voice crumbling my resolve. It has been an amazing few years. Amazing. You are perfect in almost every way. You're always there for me, you know what I need without even asking, and you care about me…you are so amazingly kind, which is why this is so hard. Please know that you did nothing to provoke this. God, this sounds so damn clichéd but this is about me, this is my fault. Those eyes, I almost can't look at you…you're such an innocent in this. I'm sorry for that. Sorry for any hurt that this may cause you but please know…I really think this is for the best. You've probably noticed that I've been a little distant. Well, there's a reason for that. I've been putting myself out there lately. I've been seeing what the world has to offer me. I've really been focused on what's best for me…and I think I finally found it. That means I'm going to have to go away for a while, maybe forever. The long-distance thing, well, it's just not going to work. I've tried to work it out, tried to figure out how it could, but I just don't see any way. So, I guess, what I really mean to say is...well...this is good-bye. I mean, part of you had to know this was coming. We both knew this couldn't last forever, this kind of thing never does.

[*Pause.*]

I'm going to go. Please don't look at me like that—Jesus, this is too hard. You are the best damn dry cleaner I've ever had and I'll never find another like you. Don't you think I know that?!!

[*Turns to go...then turns back.*]

Oh...uh...can I pick up that dress by tomorrow before five?

Makeover

Alisha Gaddis

I swear to god if you nominate me and put me on one of
those makeover shows I will kill you. I will absolutely
murder everyone involved. That is—unless I didn't die of
embarrassment. Because I would—I would die of
embarrassment.

Could you imagine—I am staring at a T. rex at the Natural
History Museum and BOOM cameras telling me I look
like an idiot. Or I am at the beach having a hotdog and
BOOM Tracey and Jeff from that TV show pop out of a
crashing wave and tell me my sarong is really So Wrong.
Or worse yet—I am picking up the kids from soccer and
multitasking as per usual and BOOM there are their faces
telling me I should be wearing a wedge!

I would murder them. Actually, I would probably be in
shock, then laugh, then cry, then be pissed. Really pissed.
Do you have to sign a release form to be on that show? Or

do they just bombard you and you have no choice about
your national exposure of shame.

Yes—I have played the scenario over and over in my head.
Almost every single time I leave the house, I check to see if
there are secret cameras in the bushes. I mean—I am a
working mom! Yoga pants can go from sleep to school to
work to date night! They have a slight sheen and nice fit on
the caboose. I cannot be expected to choose a cardigan
over my comfy college hooded sweatshirt when carting my
little shitheads to their soccer practices. I am a superwoman,
not a super well-dressed woman. I get it!

[*Beat.*] But you know…it would be kinda nice to have a
paid-for vacation like they do. You know they whisk you off
to New York for a week—no bills, no deadlines, no
homework help, no husband's emotional (and physical)
needs. Me time. I need me time. I deserve me time. And
you leave with a whole new wardrobe! How fabulous. I
wonder if I am an autumn or a spring? I bet they tell you
that. The makeup artist probably tells you all your colors.
Why do they always hire semislutty, ageless makeup artists
on those shows? Ugh. But I bet I can learn a lot from
them—don't you think!?

And I would love to have a big reveal! I would wear a slinky
dress and sling backs with drop earrings. I bet they would

give me a feathered cut—perhaps with a fringe. I have always thought I needed a good bang! Ha!

They would have the reveal at La Marabelle's. We only go there on our anniversaries—but this is a special SPECIAL occasion. Everyone will cry and bring flowers and the kids will be clean and their hair will be brushed—I didn't have to do it. And my mom will have flown in from Iowa and she won't say one shitty thing, and will even tell me, "Wow, your face looks thin!" And Tom will kiss me and be super turned on, but I will play coy and surprised but be laughing and the cameramen will love it and I will twirl around and around!

They will do an update and I will be wearing my fabulous clothes in my new office—because I will have finally gotten that promotion that I deserve at the agency. And my hair will still look flirty yet professional and I will be so happy…I really deserve it. I really deserve the makeover…

But truly that would kind of be horrible if you think about it. Could you imagine being exposed that way? Letting everyone see you like that? If they say what size I wear I would sue. I swear I would sue. Do they put cameras in the changing room? That is such a violation of privacy. I heard they do that at the Sears—I don't even go there anymore.

Ugh. Those women are pathetic. I don't need an intervention. I would be mortified. Mortified enough to murder!

Oh god—is that mustard on my under boob? I didn't even realize I leaned on my hot dog.

Manic Pixie Dream Girl

Carla Cackowski

PILAR, *twenty-two, speaks to her YouTube fans with an intimacy usually reserved for close friends and family. She is part Lolita, part Tinker Bell—both infuriating and magical. In her most vulnerable moments, both men and women find themselves under her spell.*

[PILAR *arranges herself in a chair until she feels cute and comfy. A computer screen is open in front of her. She presses the record button on the keypad.*]

Hi YouTube friends. Pilar here. It's been a few hours since I last vlogged. I missed you. I love you. I hope you love me too.

I wanted to give a quick shout out to Jacob. Jacob left a comment on my page saying, "You are the girl of my dreams." To Jacob I respond, "Thank you. You are one of the men in my dreams."

I received another comment, this time from a *female*. Nancy says, "Pilar, I feel like I know mostly everything about you. So tell us, what's inside of your purse?"

It's true, Nancy. I've shown you so much of my insides, my truth, my essence, but never the inside of my purse. So today, my friends, my lovers, my confidants—today I'm going to show you the inside of my most intimate object. I call it my Mary Poppins purse.

[PILAR *giggles like a little girl as she opens a purse as large as a piece of luggage. As she describes each object, she holds it preciously in her hands as though she were unearthing a buried treasure.*]

The first thing I have is a journal. This is where I keep my most private thoughts…I've read all of it to you in previous vlogs.

Next: lip balm. This is my favorite brand of lip balm. It keeps my lips moist so that my secrets spill out easily.

I always carry a pair of panties. Not just any panties, but my lucky panties. I never leave home without them. They're like magic fairy dust, granting the wishes of every human they come into contact with. I've never actually worn them because I don't wear panties, but I'm so relieved to have them with me when the universe presents obstacles that try to block my happy path.

And finally, my Bobbi Brown eyeliner and a picture of Gandhi.

[PILAR *kisses the picture.*]

So there you have it, Nancy…the inside of my purse. Maybe next time I'll show you the inside of my throat. I think it's pretty rad.

This afternoon, while I was planning what I was going to say about myself, I decided to pose for a new profile pic.

[PILAR *presses a button on her computer to show the audience her picture.*]

I think this outfit is okay, but what I really love about this picture is my skinny face. I like it so much that it inspired an idea for a contest! Send me the best skinny face picture of yourself, and I'll pick a winner. That person will be sent the name and address of my gynecologist so you can get a pap by the same man's hands that gave me my pap. I like to promote women's health issues when I can. That's why I dyed my hair pink this morning…because Breast Cancer Awareness month was a few months ago.

So, now I'd like to talk to you about something uber personal. Should I talk about it? I don't know, maybe I shouldn't. Should I? I don't know. I can't. But I have to! I must!

[PILAR *channels Lolita*...]

Turns out someone came into possession of a sex tape I made with my boyfriend three boyfriends ago and posted it on YouTube. I feel so violated. Like, that sex tape was for us, not for the public. Because when two people love each other, the best way for them to express it is to put a camera on a tripod and tape their most intimate moments. It got 1.4 million unique views and made the YouTube Top 10! I feel so depressed about this whole incident. I've lost my appetite and won't be able to eat at my favorite restaurant, Jamba Juice, for, like, days.

[*And then, Tinker Bell!*]

Let's go on an adventure! Let's break into houses that aren't ours! Let's splash our naked feet in Trevi Fountain while singing a Shins song! Let's stand in front of Tiffany's eating ice cream and call it breakfast! Let's do it!

[PILAR *sighs like, "It's so hard to be Pilar."*]

I hope you feel like you've gotten to know me better over the past few minutes. I definitely feel like I've gotten to know you, you marvelous human beings, you.

[PILAR *blows a kiss to her audience and closes the computer.*]

The Question

Kevin Garbee

It's always the same questions. *Got any kids? When are you guys gonna have kids? You thinkin' about having kids anytime soon?* Does it ever occur to anyone that maybe I can't have kids? That maybe my ovaries look like a hail-damaged Pinto... or there's an issue with my cervix... or my tubes are blocked or wrapped around my pancreas or something? Or that my husband has the sperm count of a seven-year-old? Hmmm? That's not the case, but I think it's pretty bold to assume that it's not the case. Or that maybe... we just don't want kids? Why can't anyone comprehend that notion? Maybe we think we'd be shitty parents. Just because we look like we'd be good parents doesn't mean you should assume we would be good parents. My mom looked the part, and she was horrid... I'm talking Hall of Fame bad. You just never know... maybe it's genetic. Or maybe we just want to live a life free from dirty diapers and runny noses and PTA meetings and T-ball practices. Is that too much to ask? Of course it is... because *Motherhood is the most selfless, life-affirming thing a person can do*...and the rest of us are just selfish pieces of shit. Then just call me selfish. Selfish shit Sara. Selfish because I want something more than a white picket fence and a country club membership. Selfish because I don't want to buy a closet full of Laura Ashley sweater sets to keep up with the Botox-ed Joneses and their spray tans. Or maybe...and I know this is a novel concept...but maybe...I just don't want to have kids... YET. Because I selfishly want to feed my soul and pursue my passions...and travel the world instead of spending every summer for fifty years at the SAME...FUCKING... LAKE HOUSE. And maybe because...and this is just me being selfish again...but maybe I just don't want to condemn my children to a life of therapy and Paxil because I never had the guts to stick my neck out and follow my dreams. Kids pick up on that shit...I'm sorry, I didn't mean to lay all that on you...I know you're busy... I'll...uh...I'll have the Cobb salad and a Diet Coke.

Never Ready

Alisha Gaddis

It has arrived. I thought I would be ready. I prepared emotionally, physically, psychologically. The whole gamut.

I knew it would happen to me. I did. It happens to everyone.

Even me.

Especially me. I mean—you know my mother.

I thought I could handle it—evidently not, though. I don't even know what to do—I mean what do you do when the inevitable happens?!?!?!

What do you do when you see a sign of your own mortality? Of life passing you by?!?

[*Beat.*]

I have a GRAY hair!

I can tell you it is nothing like I planned. I thought my first gray would be darling and cleverly hidden and maybe when I was fifty-sevenish. But oh no—it is right in the front and wiry and aggressive and not even really gray—it is snowy white. LIKE AN OLD PERSON!!

I am getting old! Really old. Seriously old. I don't even have a savings account! What am I doing with my life?!?

I should totally give up on men. Soon my whole head will be white and then my pubes will follow. (Did you know your pubes turn white!?! Disgusting!) Then who will want to be with me?!? My mom is right—I should have married Ryan from high school! Why did I think I was better than him? There is nothing wrong with being a sanitation specialist. Someone has to deal with all the shitty stuff in life—I mean, look at me for goodness sakes!

[*Breath.*]

It's fine. Everyone grays. I can totally color my hair. Easy. It says on the boxes that you just leave the dye on longer for stubborn grays. I will do that.

No one will know! It will be my own little secret. My carry-on baggage! I mean even celebrities gray, and wrinkle…and rot…and die.

OH GOD!! I am going to die soon! Die with a bad dye job, broke and all alone!

[*Beat.*]

Really? You can't even notice?...Well, I suppose I could just pluck it out.

In Hot Water

Arthur M. Jolly

Adapted from The Four Senses of Love.

MELITA, *a woman born with no sense of taste, is at a support group for the sensory deprived.*

If you're blind, everyone knows it. You can't hide blind. But taste? Damn right, I try and fit in.

Think I wanna go around telling people I have no taste— no taste at all? If I'm out with friends, I'll get tea—just to, you know. D'you know the nutritional value of tea? Exactly the same as hot water. Two bucks for dirty brown color. But I'll spend it.

[*Beat.*]

Once, this girl Julie—I knew her from the gym, we saw each other all the time. You know—early friendship, but real. I mean, I could see being her bridesmaid, down the road. We coulda been...Well, we went out, me and her and her boyfriend Rick. Rick keeps saying, "You gotta try this place, you gotta try this coffee place"—and we all pile in his ratty BMW, and I'm wedged in the back with my knees up under my chin, and we get to this little cafe, and Rick says hi to the guy behind the counter—and it's like this whole show he's putting on for Julie, cause really—it's a coffee place...you meet, you talk. He brings me over this something something something latte. And it was warm water with a faintly slimy foam and a little grit on top—cinnamon. Like very fine sawdust. And he's all: "How is it? It's the best, right? What'd I tell ya, the best." Why is he asking if he's already got the answer? So I'm sitting there, and I started playing with the foam. I would put my tongue in it—and then roll the cinnamon between my tongue and the roof of my mouth. Texture—gritty, sandpaper rolling.

[*She starts miming it—getting more and more into it. Lots of foam-licking tongue action.*]

Foam bubbles bursting, little points of contact, the tip of my tongue delving into the foam, the hot water, the temperature between the hot and the warm foam and the cool of the edge of the cup....Playing with the foam... feeling the grit...

[*She's getting totally carried away. She stops dead, looks up from her imaginary cup.*]

Rick was staring at me. Julie got so mad. Screaming at me, said I was a...all kinds of things. [*Beat.*]

I was just playing with the foam. Hot water. That's why they use that phrase—getting in to hot water.... That was the last time I saw her.

[*Beat.*]

Rick called a whole bunch of times.

Albinoid I Am

Hasalyn Modine

I found out today, I am albino. [*A beat.*]

I'm not joking. [*Another, awkward beat.*]

I can hear what you're thinking: "But she doesn't have red eyes? Does she?" "She's lying." "I've seen albino turtles on Animal Planet…all albinos have red eyes and feather hair."

Well, you're wrong. A red eye does not an albino make. Of course I didn't know this until today, when I found my people.

Flashback now, to me, age five, diagnosed by my pediatric ophthalmologist as "almost albino."

My CRAZY mother—oh you think YOUR mom is crazy? You think ALL moms are crazy? DID YOUR MOTHER SHOW UP TO YOUR HIGH SCHOOL BAND CONCERT WEARING LINGERIE?!?!

I digress…my crazy mother diagnosed my albinism LONG before finding said pediatric ophthalmologist…it only took her eight quacks to find one who would agree with her.

To be fair. I look nothing like my mother. Or my father. I mostly look like my stepmother, who I thought for years was really my mother, who only gave me up to my crazy mother because she felt sorry for her. Dammit…I keep losing focus.

Did you know that most albinos are legally blind? Including me.

Hence, the ophthalmologist.

So upon the diagnosis of almost albinism, I was sentenced to death by way of photo-gray lenses. Do you know what they are? Have you ever seen a mug shot of a creepy trucker with tinted glasses? Those are most likely photo-gray. No, they never really untint. Yes, they are always brown and creepy.

My father denounced said pediatric ophthalmologist (and my mother)—I should mention, they're divorced—and purchased ANOTHER set of untinted glasses for me to wear on the weeks I was at his house.

Evidence of the façade that lasted for six years thereafter is my double set of school pictures: tinted creeper child photos at my mom's, and (same outfit) normal lenses at my dad's.

It really is a miracle I'm not a sociopath.

By the time my mom learned about my second set of glasses, I already had contacts, and she was busy diagnosing me with extra bones in my feet (she almost convinced a podiatrist to put casts on both feet to "calm the inflammation" before my dad intervened and bought me Birkenstocks to help my arches).

For nearly twenty-five years, my almost albinism has been my father's family joke.

Until today, I went to the eye doctor. I can never seem to get a 20/20 prescription, and I was hoping she'd give me some glasses to put over my contacts so I could see street signs again. Or for the first time.

This particular doctor was a specialist—she's used to seeing weird eyes. But when she saw mine, she started giggling. Giddy like.

An eye doctor laughing, when you're helpless with dilated pupils, is somewhat disconcerting…so I asked, "What the hell is so funny?"

She said, "Well, I've just only seen eyes like yours in textbooks. Never in real life." [*A beat.*] "You know, ocular albinism."

(What. The Fuck.)

"Because," she said, "your retinas sparkle."

[*A beat.*] [*Blank stare, jaw drops.*]

"No one ever told you?" the eye doctor asked. [*A beat.*] "When I look at normal eyes, the retina is like a piece of cardboard. Your retinas are like Swiss cheese. The light shines through and makes them sparkle. Red-eyed albinos' eyes quiver in the light, yours just shine."

That's right everyone...my eyes sparkle like a Twilight Vampire.

Becoming an albinoid, as we like to call ourselves, was the best day of my life. There is something really liberating about never having to try to be tan again. Also, I'm a genetic goddess. A lot of shit had to happen for my eyes to twinkle like they do. It's a shame I have to keep this secret from my mother...I wouldn't want her to know she was right.

Always Awkward

Jessica Glassberg

From the one-woman show
Most Likely To...?
Written and originally performed by
Jessica Glassberg.

JESSICA *is a Jewish 26-year-old living in Los Angeles*
wondering what to do with the rest of her life.

Do you remember middle school? Have you blocked out
the braces and acne and bad perm too? If you think Los
Angeles is bad, think back to middle school. That's where
you really learn to hate your body. I still have nightmares
about going to buy my first bra.

I come home and tell my mom that I really think it's time
for me to get a bra...I think I'm ready...I'm twenty-six.

No, I'm in the sixth grade, standing in the dressing room
with my mom and Gertrude...the grandma-like sales

associate who helps the preteens pick out their first bras. My mom just keeps saying how I don't need a bra.

(Jessica as her mom.) Honey, there's nothing, there. You've got little pebbles. Do you think it's fun carrying these double Ds around? [*To Gertrude.*] Gertrude, could you get my Jessie a training bra? You have to "train" them. [*Laugh.*] [*To Jessica.*] Come on sweetie...try it on...(then) turn around and show us how it looks. What are you embarrassed? I'm your mother...I changed your diapers, I've seen you naked with poopie and pee-pee all over you...

I carried you around for nine months...stretch marks... Do you know the kind of stretch marks I have to deal with every day?...These don't go away...here [*Picks up shirt.*] here...right across here and up here...look at me...You see this?...I did this for you and you won't turn around in a bra? [*Crying.*]...

You're my baby. I know that you're all grown up with your perm and braces like a big girl...but you're still my little baby and you always will be...I knew you were special from the moment the doctor delivered you [*Turning angry.*] after over twenty-four HOURS of labor and the pain and the pushing...you took your good sweet time coming out, but I went through it for you! And you won't let me see you in a bra? Come on, turn around. There we go. [*To*

Gertrude.] Oh Gertrude, this one isn't good. It makes her look all pointy, we want them to look round…I mean, pointy is better than nonexistent, but come on. Ooh, ooh, I have a thought…maybe something with padding? At least if she's going to get a bra and she doesn't have anything to fill it with, the bra can already come fully assembled, ready with it's own little boobies and everything.

(Jessica.) I'm much more comfortable with myself now. I have an okay body. I mean I'm not as self-conscious as I was in sixth grade. [*Uncomfortable laugh and look at chest.*] They're normal…sure…nothing too big or really THAT small…but average…a solid C…well, a small C…a large B?

Christian Summer Camp Theater Director

Jenny Yang

It's 2005. As a child, CHRIS *was never the devout Christian her mother wanted her to be. She had sex as a teenager and later turned to Christianity to cleanse herself of the guilt. Now, fresh out of college, she considers herself a born-again Christian. Unfortunately, she's sexually repressed and surprises herself when sexuality comes up in unexpected ways. She is applying for a job as an acting teacher and theater director for a California Central Valley Christian bible camp. In this monologue,* CHRIS *is in a job interview with the camp director.*

I came to my calling in theater the same way I came to my relationship with Jesus. Through Passion...with a capital P. More *Passion of the Christ*, less *Passions* the soap opera on NBC.

My Christian Theater teaching philosophy is Recitation of
Verse, Expression of His Spirit.

I spent the last three years taking classes at Fresno
Christian Academy and leading theater workshops with the
Youth Fellowship at my home church in Biola. Our group
just wrapped up a production of *Jesus Christ Superstar*...I
did play the costarring role of Mary Magdalene, just in the
case there wasn't a high schooler with the gravitas to pull
off such a complex role...you know, Mary was a Jew.
Who'd want to burden a child with that confusion?...
Apparently it was all the Jews' fault that Jesus died anyway,
right? [*Laughs.*] That's the reason for the two months right
there. [*Points to the resume.*] It was not a paid job, but it was
great because I could focus on my Youth Fellowship work,
full-time. I am so incredibly blessed to be raised by a
God-fearing mother who has been supporting me while I
focus on developing my talents in Christian theater. There
isn't a single day when my mother doesn't praise the lord
and me for taking what she considers devil's activities like
alternate-nostril breathing and squatted spinal stretching
to do God's work. [*Whispers.*] Mother believes acting
warm-up exercises are akin to...[Says like it's a dirty word.]
"yoga." But we know better, don't we?

There is just something so breathtaking about a high
school senior's ability to get past the temptations of the

flesh by controlling their own senses through what I like to call "sense-memory prayer."

I have them sit in their seats comfortably and close their eyes while they listen closely to the sound of my voice as I hypnotically lead them through a meditative prayer to teach them how to control the sensations of their body. If I may...

[*Speaks breathlessly like a phone sex commercial and closes her eyes to demonstrate.*]

Right now...breathe in through your nose and slowly out with your mouth. Feel the cool air rush past the tender surface of your lip hole. Keep them moist as you pull in a deep swallow of air...And out. Now, take special notice anywhere in your body where there may be tension. Focus your mind's eye on that place in your body and breathe in through your mouth and hold that breath...until you can feel that oxygen reaching this point of tension, massaging it to...release...breathe out."

[*Opens eyes and nods. Pleased with herself.*]

If you will have me as your theater director, I would love to bring on my dear friend Gary Cochran part-time to help me with music. I'd like to insist, in fact, because I consider us a packaged deal. Gary has this incredible way of sucking you into bible verses through gospel-inspired but more pop-slash-R&B-contemporary stylings that really draw in our youth. I consider him the Chris Brown of Christ, but less "Take You Down" Chris Brown and more...well... "I Believe I Could Fly" if he was R. Kelly. But without the scandal and sin...of both men. Women must be respected...Gary is just an amazing innovator.

And believe me, I've discovered one can both innovate and worship Christ. All of our vocal warm-ups are essentially recitations of the twenty-five most popular bible verses.

[*While singing ascending scales.*]

Romans, chapter 12, verse 1: Therefore, I urge you, brothers, in view of God's mercy, to offer your bodies as living sacrifices, holy and pleasing to God—this is your spiritual act of worship.

Jesus created theater to present pageantry worthy of the physical embodiment of Christ's glory. I have prayed on this and I believe Jesus understands that like the beauty of stained glass in a house of worship, we can bring together the body of Christ through sophisticated lighting design and glitter.

Mr. Carney. Christian theater is serious business. Deep down I believe it is my calling. And I would be so humbled if you could offer me the chance to share the Lord's work as your new theater director.

An Act of Change

Tanner Efinger

Would you like to see a show, ma'am?...Hello, sir, would you like a flier for a show?...Hi guys! We're on every day at 3:15 p.m....No? That's okay. Hello sir...Oh, headphones.

[*She jumps around, motions to the man with the headphones, and then starts to laugh at herself.*]

Just kidding. But really, would you like to see my show?

[*She trips over a man sitting on the street.*]

Oh excuse me sir, I didn't see you sitting there. Spare a little change? Sure. Why not. I've got fifty cents. Sorry, it's not much. But you also have to take a flier.

Hello ma'am, pity me and take a flier. Will you take this piece of paper to make me feel better about myself? NO?! [*To the homeless man.*] What is wrong with people? Handing out fliers for your own off-off-off Broadway one-woman musical is the most demoralizing, dehumanizing—okay, fine, well maybe not the MOST dehumanizing thing…I suppose I could be asking for fifty cents from starving actors—okay, well not actually starving. I complain too much. I hate New York City. Would you like a flier for my one-woman musical?…I hate being an actress…[*To the homeless man.*] But really? What else am I going to do with myself? Would you like a flier, sir? I can't wait tables, because I'm clumsy. I can't work in an office, because computers give me a headache. My hands are too soft for hard labor and my ankles are too weak to be an athlete. I haven't the patience for childcare, the stomach for nursing, the compassion for nonprofit—Would you like a flier, sir?—or the sensibility for fashion. ALL I HAVE IS MY TALENT! It's a curse. [*Beat.*] May I sit with you?

[*She sits with the homeless man.*]

I keep having this dream. I'm standing on a stage and a huge audience is sitting in anticipation, on the edge of their seat…expecting me to do something…to do anything. I try to speak but I have no voice. I…I try to dance, but my legs are locked. I try to breathe, but my lungs are locked. The audience is getting restless now. Bored. I see someone leave in the back. And I start to panic. And since I can't speak, or dance, or breathe…I…this sounds ridiculous…

but I start to float. My feet leave the ground and I just float away. The ceiling opens and I float breathlessly into the night sky. The theater is like an ant as I float up to the black night above. And up here there's no need to sing, or dance, or be…everything has changed. Change? Maybe that's what I need. A little change.

[*She looks out and holds out her hand.*]

Spare some change? A little change, sir?

How to Protect Your Cub in the Wild

Alisha Gaddis

From a column in the all-female online magazine Say Something Funny…B*tch.

I had a traumatizing run-in with the Easter Bunny this year. I was with my daughter, who is now eight and is at the delicate age where you either write Santa beautiful letters begging for ponies and fairy wings, or you become a whore. Obviously, I have to steer her in the right direction.

We were walking in the mall (and don't judge me for being in the mall—they have a free indoor playground, other children, and an espresso bar—I get malls now). This particular day at the mall, we were on a mission—we were going to see the Easter Bunny. A really big event. We waited in the long line with squirmy children, overworked nannies, and a few mothers with sky-high heels (this is Los

Angeles, after all). We finally got our turn. My daughter was elated. She ran up, gave him a squeeze, then the EB bounced her a little too long for my liking on his lap. We took some pictures. Then happily skipped off to the playground.

Best. Mom. Ever.

When it was time to leave an hour later, we had to walk through the food court to get to the parking garage.

There was the Easter Bunny…eating chow mein…with his head off.

His head off!

The Easter Bunny was headless eating chow mein! The pimply, scrawny teenager could have cared less. Children were crying, dreams were being shattered, little boys were getting aggressive!

Obviously, my first, and only, instinct was to run next to the gyro station and scream, "FIRE!"

I dove over my daughter's head, ducked, and rolled. Mothers started screaming, businessmen took one last bite of their hotdog on a stick before waddling off, and the

Easter Bunny—the Easter Bunny put back on his head and hopped away.

We hid in the Old Navy while the authorities tried to figure out what hooligan called a false fire.

They never found the perpetrator.

But that will teach the Easter Bunny. Another pure heart saved.

Forgive Me Father

Hasalyn Modine

FORGIVE ME FATHER: For I have sinned.

I may or may not have intentionally thrown a tennis ball with my dog's chucker at a mutant child who was being very nasty to his family.

This happened in the summer of 2009.

The child may or may not have been riding a bicycle with said family. My dog MAY or MAY NOT have knocked said child from said bike in an effort to fetch—as black labs are wont to do.

The child may or may not have yelled, "MOMMY, SHE HIT ME," as it laid on the ground post bike fall.

I may or may not have yelled back, "YOU DESERVED IT FOR BEING SUCH AN ASSHOLE TO YOUR FAMILY!" to the child.

It was a dark moment. I'm not proud. That's why I'm here.

I also need to confess about a recent incident at a movie theater.

When people laugh obnoxiously in the theater—usually with a mouth full of popcorn and/or Milk Duds—I am prone to mimic their laughs.

Loudly.

Like this:

HAHAHAHAHAHAAHAHAHAHAHAHAH. [*This should be a terrible laugh noise—loud and piercing and awful.*]

When those people laugh at nonfunny moments in the film—and they ALWAYS DO—I may laugh back louder, more obnoxiously.

If ever I'm asked to go to dinner and a movie, I decline. I know how it will end. He'll hate me forever after he sees what I do.

That's why I need your forgiveness.

But really, when things aren't funny, you ought not laugh.

Fluff and Fold

Moreen Littrell

I don't know if this has ever happened to you, but a few months ago I noticed my underwear started disappearing. And these were my GOOD underwear. My special occasion underwear, if you know what I'm talking about.

And my first thought was, "Those fucking fluff and fold people stole 'em." So the next time I went to my dry cleaner I said, "Um, so, I'm missing some of my underwear…" And she says, "Oh no. We no take yo undehweh. Yo sure you no leave someweh?"

What like I'm a traveling circus ho? "Ladies and Gentlemen: in the big tent is the Traveling Circus Ho. Watch how she makes her underwear disappear."

"No," I told her, "I've looked everywhere. There's no other place they could be. This is the only place they GO." Now I didn't want to ride Ms. Wong too hard for a confession, because part of me is sympathetic to the fact that we are living in tough times and if she needs to steal my underwear to put fortune cookies on the table, I get it. So I kind of just look over her head towards the back, which is my way of communicating to her that I know what you're up to. I know you've got an underwear chop shop. And it's a great idea. Because my underwear would make great curtains. They WOULD. Not all of them, but these...yeah. These would.

But today, after weeks of telling everyone to be on the lookout for couture cotton-paneled curtains made by Wong Cleaners, I found my missing underwear. They were in my overnight bag, which was no longer an overnight bag since I broke up with my boyfriend. Sadly my overnight bag is now just a bag.

Anyway, I have decided that I cannot tell Mrs. Wong that I found my underwear. Because if I tell her that I found them, I will never be able to accuse her again. And then, when she steals my premium denim jeans for a curtain valance to put duck sauce on the table, she will say, "I no take yo jeans. You thought I take yo undehweh. You can go fluff yousef."

So if anyone asks, the curious case of the missing underwear remains curious.

Yoga

Alisha Gaddis

Yoga schomoga. Yoga really isn't an ancient doctrine you know. I mean, maybe it has ancient roots, but so do the Masons—do they even exist anymore?!?! Yoga has become out of control lately, and I will not be a part of it! It is just a hipster fad of stretching and sweat and sports bras and pants named for the activity.

Yoga pants—geez. More people wear yoga pants to Sunday brunch than actually go to yoga class! Posers.

I hate yogis.

But I HATE yoga teachers even more.

I feel like everyone around me who can't figure out what they are going to do with their lives are studying to be yoga teachers.

I am tired of saying, "I'm sorry your theater/sociology/
African studies degree didn't work out—that's amazing that
you are teaching the new vinyasa flow class at Yummy
Tummy Yoga!"

What I really want to say is, "Get a real job and an
apartment of your own!"

I am not bitter that I have a nine to five. I love the job
security I have as an executive assistant. After another six
months, I qualify for insurance through a separate
provider. You can't argue with that! I am so glad I gave up
my silly dream of being a writer. What is a writer anyway?
Everyone is a writer now that the Internet exists. I can have
a blog right now and get a billion hits and become a
sensation and then be on *Good Morning USA* and then my
mother will finally be proud of me!

But I don't. I don't need that. And I don't need to open my
hip flexors, goddamit!

I don't need to go into a stinky room after a full day in my
open-concept office, listening to my incompetent boss
(who thinks we are friends, I might add) and strip down to
Downward-Facing Dog.

I don't need to Ommmm my way to Bliss—I already know that my bliss is recorded in the form of a one-hour crime drama waiting for me on my DVR.

I don't want to eat vegan and don't want to activate my third eye!!!

And I most certainly do NOT want to do yoga. So please, take your free introductory class flier back and shove it where the vinyasa don't shine.

[*Beat.*]

Namaste to you, too.

The Write Way

Kelly Moll

HAPPY NEW YEAR!! I have come to the conclusion—I want to be a writer. Start the New Year off by doing what I am really supposed to do—writing! Yes. A WRITER! Only…is there anything left that hasn't been written about? All of my trials and tribulations—all of my best shit—seems to already be on paper in some form or another.

To highlight a few:

1. Hideous divorce followed by quest to reclaim and rejuvenate life—Elizabeth Gilbert pretty much cornered the market on that one and put a cherry on top by having Julia Roberts play her in *Eat Pray Love*. Nice work, ma'am.

2. The unbearable heartache and persisting love that comes with having a sibling with a serious illness and disability. I could write volumes about the amazing

being who is my brother. Unfortunately, these themes have been obligingly covered (and made into a movie) by Jodi Picoult in *My Sister's Keeper*, along with several other wonderful books (oh, the angst of it all!).

3. My hilarious eardrum incident already described in brilliant detail by Stephen King—well done, sir.

4. Even my foul-mouthed snarkiness has already been done better by another Minnesota writer, Diablo Cody. If only I'd had the balls to be a stripper ten years ago when I had a washboard stomach (strictly for writing material, of course).

5. And my gigantic, enmeshed, passive-aggressive, yet loving and well-intentioned family? Well, I could swear Jonathan Franzen may have moved into my parents' basement while writing part of that amazing book, *The Corrections* (my favorite).

All of my blunders in general (like the time I got hit by an Isuzu Rodeo while running on the River Road—long story) are a bit Bridget Jones-esque, and I'm quite sure the general population could not stomach another floundering thirtysomething (oh Christ, she was probably in her twenties). Take away the British accent, and it's a pretty hard sell.

I am aware that because I wasted my formative years on a popularity quest, my college years on drinking, and my twenties (the cutest and most vibrant decade of my life) on a salty, depressing, juvenile marriage—that I am a little late to the party of putting pen to paper. Sure I can turn a phrase with some manner of witty vocab—man, do I love a good bit of phraseology. A colorful, well-played sentence can really put a smile on my face. I love words—I love when they are well chosen and surprising and poignant and thoughtful. I can get lost in words and live there for days. But mine are short bursts—stunted.

Where is the story? WHERE IS MY STORY!?!?!

It's like I'm writing snappy jingles instead of an overture. Give me characters, give me plot and conflict!

Is my lack of story my story? A writer's life is so complicated!

[*Beat.*]

Oh god. My New Year's resolution should have just been to join the gym.

Thoughtful Mourner

Carla Cackowski

BARBARA, *in her forties, is shopping with her friend in the accessories department of a high-end department store.* BARBARA *is hypersensitive to how she is perceived by others.*

I can't decide which sunglasses to go with. Linda, which do you think? Linda. You're not paying attention. Which glasses do you think? Large frames...

[BARBARA *tries on glasses. She then switches to—*]

Or small? It's like Audrey Hepburn versus...I don't know. Yoko Ono? It *does* make a difference. Sure it does. I think the large frames look better on me, but if I wear the large, people might not see my tears at the funeral. Yes, I know how that sounds, Linda. But the way that it sounds is not the way that I *mean* for it to sound. What I mean to say is, I'm going to cry. I want to make sure Donna sees me crying so that she doesn't think that I don't care that her

parents have died. It's important that she *sees* that I care.
So, which do you think, Linda? Small? Yes, I think you're
right.

It's all just such a nightmare, isn't it? It's like a horror
movie. She goes to bed at night, she's got two parents, she
wakes up in the morning and they're both gone! It's
horrible, don't you think? Yes, you're absolutely right, just
horrible...I still don't understand the details. Skiing.
That's all I know. But both of them at once, so, did they ski
into a tree at the same time? Holding hands? Perhaps they
fell off the lift? Either way, it's devastating. Oh, I like these!

[BARBARA *tries on another pair of glasses.*]

You're right. They're terrible.

[BARBARA *takes off the glasses immediately.*]

I almost forgot to tell you! Look, this is something I
haven't told anyone yet, so please don't repeat it. Do you
promise me? Swear. Swear it on your mother's grave. Ugh,
that's inappropriate. Okay, swear on MY mother's grave.
That bitch. Get it? Okay, still inappropriate? Sorry...Yes, I
know you won't tell anyone. The day before it happened,
Donna and I were in the office together and her phone was
ringing off the hook—please don't repeat this—her phone

was ringing off the hook and it was all these people—clients—who wanted to buy life insurance policies from her! She sold five life insurance policies the day before her parents died in a mysterious and horrific accident that had something to do with skiing! Isn't that bizarre? The whole situation is like a Stephen King novel. You know, like *The Shining*, except, you know, not taking place in a hotel...I shouldn't, what? I shouldn't tell people, what? Oh. About her selling all those life insurance policies? That's why I asked you not to repeat it, because I'm not going to tell anyone. Do you think we should get hats? Well, we might be standing outside for a while. I mean this isn't your typical funeral. There are two bodies. It could take a while to bury both.

[BARBARA *tries on hats.*]

I already hate funerals, but two at once! It's almost too much to bear. Do you think she considered burying them on separate days? I mean, it might be less stressful for the guests if she had done something like that...No, you're right. It would just drag it out. I think a hat would be nice. Which do you think, large?

[BARBARA *places a large-rimmed hat on her head. And then immediately replaces it with—*]

Or larger? Yes, you're completely right. Large is enough...
I stopped by her house last night to drop off a lasagna.
Well, I figured she might be hungry. It's a nice thing to do,
you know, to drop off food for people in mourning. I
wanted her to know that I was thinking of her and that I'm
upset about her loss. But I got there and she already had six
lasagnas! Her daughter answered the door and, don't tell
anyone I told you this because it sounds paranoid, but I
swear she rolled her eyes at me! She answered the door and
I was teary eyed and said, "I'm sorry for your family's loss,"
and I handed her the lasagna I spent two hours making and
she mumbled, "Thank you," or something like that, and as
she turned, I swear, she rolled her eyes! Yes, you're
completely right—teenagers can be so rude! No, I didn't
even get to see her. Her daughter said she was lying down.
What a waste. I really wanted to tell her how sorry I was in
person. Now my sympathies are just one of six anonymous
lasagnas sitting in a refrigerator. Oh, this hat is navy blue,
not black. Is that okay? Or is it not okay? Linda. Linda!
Focus! This is important. Will she know how sad I am if I
wear a navy blue hat instead of a black one? It's just so hard
to be noticed at a funeral, isn't it?

On Trend

Rebekah Tripp

Wha wha what??? I thought half shirts went out with Richard Simmons, ladies! Yet...today, at one of my favorite North Hollywood eateries...I come face to face with this grotesquely amputated tank top. The other day...I saw a super trendy gal wearing an asymmetrically cut belly shirt. Let me just tell you...no matter how you cut the fabric...you can't trick me...I know a filthy stinking belly shirt when it ignorantly stares me in the face.

Mind you...the ladies wearing these shirts were fit enough to wear them. I didn't vurp (that's a vomit burp) because the piece of clothing showed a cottage cheesy midriff (by the by...my midriff can look a little cottage cheesy from time to time, so I know of that which I speak)...I vurped because this style just shouldn't be allowed to be worn...much like the hugely controversial and decidedly unattractive jean legging known as the

Jegging. The reasoning behind my dislike for the belly shirt is sound…everyone that wears a belly shirt looks f'in stupid.

IT IS A FACT.

So Monica—(Wake-up call, David Hasselhoff…That look doesn't work for anyone—not the Hoff . . . and not you)—I don't ever want to know if you have an innie or an outie. I could care less if you have abs of steel. Put an actual damn shirt on and don't alter it to show me your bowlful of jelly…it's freakin' gross and I don't want to see it. Thanks a bunch.

But that color is nice…maybe they have it in my size…

End of Innocence

Alisha Gaddis

Well, I experienced the end of romance. The final stop on the love boat. The straw that broke this camel's back.

My husband bought me Intense Wrinkle Cream. INTENSE. WRINKLE. CREAM.

[*Beat.*]

Honestly, I think I am in shock. Don't get me wrong—when he came home with a beautiful little bag wrapped from my favorite department store and a silly smile—I thought he had finally taken the hint and bought me some quality perfume. But ooooohhhhhh NO! When I tore past the pretty tissue and realized that staring back at me was what he ACTUALLY thinks about me—I felt like I was sucker punched with the one-two switcheroo.

I was totally baffled. I didn't know what to say. But I didn't have to—I just started crying...and crying...and yelling...and then more crying.

I think the tears came from mourning my youth, mourning that I could no longer be in denial at the loss of my youth, but mostly I was freaking pissed that my husband actually thought this was a good gift!

Then, it really did sink in. He bought me INTENSE WRINKLE CREAM. And presented it to me with pleasure and a sense of urgency. He acknowledges that I am getting old, but wants to preserve my youth. With this "gift" he is trying to keep my current youthful glow that is fading quicker than a bad spring-break sunburn. He is basically begging me to stay forever young!

And I can't! I cannot stay forever young. It is scientifically impossible.

I don't understand, though—I thought we were aging *together*. I mean, I accept his growing little bald spot and gray nose hairs. We laugh together at our recently acquired lactose intolerance and achy morning bones! Neither one of us can eat dinner after ten, and we most certainly don't want to go on a dirty-thirty pub crawl! I thought we were in this together!?!?!

Why did HE buy ME the cream?!

During a semipassionate romp in the sheets yesterday, he even dramatically whispered, "I will always remember you like this."…

What the hell does that mean?!?!?

I will always remember you like this. Why does he need to remember me like this? Am I getting worse by the moment? He needs to remember this exact time because all other times after this are on the decline?

Why does HE keep reminding ME about my soon-to-be glory days? I thought my laugh lines were friendly and inviting, but apparently I'm turning into an old hag! We better Instagram my good looks now, because soon I will need shellac to cover my age spots and should only be photographed in soft light!

[*Beat.*]

Do you think he is going to cheat on me with a younger woman? A little young thing without semisagging breasts, whose teeth have yet to be stained by coffee and hands aren't showing their age?

Do you think he still loves me?

I just...I just thought we were in this together. This aging. This life.

[*Beat.*]

I must admit, though—I did start using the cream. It works. Goddammit—it works.

Open-Faced Turkey Sandwich

Alisha Gaddis

Yes, I will have the reuben sandwich, extra pickles, with the fries and a Diet Coke. My husband's in the bathroom, but he would like your open-faced turkey sandwich. Just the way it is. With milk. Whatever percentage you have.

You married? Yeah? Then you will totally get this. He is on this big quest—the quest for the ultimate open-faced turkey sandwich. It started as a joke—he would order it here and there, our friends would laugh at dinner parties about it…then he just became…obsessed. Starting Googling diners across America. We would use our weekends to truck about to different locations. He even started a Facebook Fan Page room! We aren't even from here—we live in Topeka, Kansas, for god sakes.

I have mixed feelings about it—not the sandwich—my husband's sudden zealousness—I am so tired of driving to

Timbuktu so he can sample a random café's take on Thanksgiving dinner between two slices of bread. I am also tired of him posting photos of each and every sandwich he eats. It is like he is cataloging all of his memories based on which day had stuffing and which day had excessive gravy.

I am usually in the background of every single photo—blurry. You can usually see my hands—wedding ring and all! In the background of his life. But I am sitting there! I ordered a bloody sandwich, too (occasionally a salad, depending on which fad diet I am on)—but why doesn't he want me in that photo? Am I not as pretty, as juicy, as much of a prize as his freaking sandwich?!?!?

But mostly, I am just glad THIS is his midlife crisis. That's what I really think it is when it comes down to it. Here is this grown man—trying to discover the most Ultimate Open- Faced Turkey Sandwich ever—what childhood trauma is he trying to work through? Does he want to hang on to his youth when there is anticipation of the holidays—Christmas and Santa, snow days and laughter lingering around the corner!? Does he want to feel free?

Or does he want to find real meaning in his life? He is searching. Aren't we all really? Searching for meaning? I get it. I understand. I have been in a book club, a knitting club, a gardening team, studied Mandarin, and tried to do a ceramics class all in the last year! Nothing stuck. I admire his lust for the prize. His gumption to sticking with this. The need for the perfect bite of life. It's become his thing. Our friends Paul and Ruthie got him a T-shirt that says, "Gobbling Life Up—the quest for the best open-faced turkey sandwich." It was meant to be a joke, but he wears it every time we go out. Every. Single. Time.

[*Beat.*] I am just glad he isn't having an affair. Because let's call a spade a spade. Just like cigarettes are the gateway to marijuana and midlife crisis motorcycles are the gateway to sex with your significantly younger secretary or the stay-at-home slightly sexy lady next door—midlife crisis hits and it hits hard. If my husband happens to have a hankering for turkey—I am gonna support him. I will sit right here and be blurry in the background. Because at least we are here together, right? At least he isn't having an affair. He doesn't have time for an affair—too much turkey out there in the world. And, at least we have each other. Right? Gobbling life up!

Oh—did I tell you no mayo? 'Cause that's where I draw the line.

Contributors

These funny monologues were written by actually funny people.

Here is their business of funny:

ALISHA GADDIS is a Latin Grammy Award–winning performer, producer, humorist, and writer based in Los Angeles, California. Born in the heart of the Midwest to a champion football coach father and cheerful kindergarten teacher mother, Alisha is a graduate of New York University's Tisch (Stella Adler Theatre) and the University of Sydney, Australia. Her writing has appeared on sites including College Candy, Comediva, Babble, and in *GOOD* magazine. As a stand-up comic, she has headlined throughout the nation at venues including the World Famous Comedy Store, New York Comedy Club, and Gotham Comedy Club. As a performer, Alisha has appeared on Broadway, at Second City Hollywood, Improv Olympic West, Upright Citizens Brigade, the Sydney Opera House, the Comedy Central Stage, and has toured nationally with her critically acclaimed solo shows (playing multiple festivals including

Los Angeles Comedy Festival, New York Fringe Festival, Heartland Comedy Fest, and more). Alisha is the founder of the prolific Proletarian Improv Troupe, and has performed in more than twenty different improv troupes throughout the country. As an actress, she has appeared on television shows for MTV, CBS, Univision, NBC, and more—receiving a Producer's Guild of America nomination for best comedic ensemble. She can be seen weekly on the Emmy Award–winning PBS show *Friday Zone* with Lishy Lou and Lucky Too. As a voice-over artist, Alisha can be heard voicing numerous ad campaigns, commercials, and apps. Alisha is the founder of Say Something Funny…B*tch—the hit all-female online magazine and stand-up show of the same name. Also, Alisha is cofounder and performer (with her husband) for the first children's band from America ever to win a Latin Grammy, and *USA Today*'s Best Kid's group— Lucky Diaz and the Family Jam Band. Their music has topped the charts at Sirius XM and was featured on NPR's *All Things Considered* and in *People* magazine as the number one family album of the year. Alisha has been named "the face of kindie music" by several publications, including *New York Magazine*. The band's song "Falling" was featured as Coca-Cola's national summer ad campaign screened at movie theaters across the country. Alisha lives with her husband, songwriter Lucky Diaz, and stepdaughter in a magical cottage in Los Angeles. *www.alishagaddis.com* and *www.luckydiazmusic.com*

JAMIE BRUNTON is a Los Angeles–based comedian, writer, and actress. Her writing has been featured on various websites including Say Something Funny…B*tch, aloneinaforest, and Comediva. She was the writer and host of Comedy Time's *Ladies Night Out* and her stand-up has appeared on NUVOtv's *Stand Up and Deliver*. She is also the creator of "Red Wine, Cats & Recipes," a column on Say Something Funny…B*tch and an official Los Angeles Comedy Festival selection that mixes stand-up, sketch comedy, and cooking. Whether she's reading the audience their teen horoscopes, telling jokes as a 1920s flapper, or simply confessing that all her furniture has come from the trash, Jamie Brunton has made a name for herself as a prolific and highly imaginative performer. In easily one of the best moments of Jamie's life, Dana Gould compared her inventive style of comedy to Albert Brooks. She also really likes wine.

CARLA CACKOWSKI is a writer, improviser, and actor currently living and creating in Los Angeles. As an ensemble member of the comedy troupe The Second City, Carla spent a year touring the world performing improvisation and sketch comedy abroad Norwegian Cruise Lines. Carla has written and performed four comedic solo shows that have toured Los Angeles's theater circuit: *Girl Overboard*; *Sister Mary Liar*; *Skinny Faces, Quacking Ducks*; and *Sweatlodged*. Sweatlodged was an official selection of the 2013 United Solo Festival in New York City. Other festivals Carla has performed in include the L.A. Indie Improv Festival, Del Close Marathon (NYC), San Francisco Sketchfest, Phoenix Improv Festival, Chicago Improv Festival, and Out of Bounds Comedy Festival in Austin, Texas. She is a member of SAG-AFTRA and, as a voice-over artist, has been featured on television shows such as *iCarly*, *Pretty Little Liars*, and *Cougar Town*. Carla is a faculty member at The Second City in Los Angeles, teaching improvisation to both teens and adults. She is also a proud member of The Solo Collective, a theater company of five unique solo artists devoted exclusively to one-person performance. *www.thesolocollective.com* and *www.carlacackowski.com*

TANNER EFINGER is primarily an improv comedian. He has worked with ComedySportz (NYC), Bruised Fruits (NYC), Proletarian Improv (L.A.), Oxford Imps (UK), and many others. He has taught improv at schools including Phillips Academy Andover, Phillips Exeter Academy, Princeton University, Golden Performing Arts (L.A.), and Charterhouse School (UK). As he types this, he is performing to sold-out audiences at the Edinburgh Fringe 2013. He has written for many blogs and magazines, has written two screenplays and one stage play, and is now working on his first novel.

KEVIN GARBEE is a comedian, humorist, raconteur, and redundant person based in Los Angeles. As is obligatory in these bios, he wants you to know that he lives with his wife and two cats. To learn not much more, please visit his website. *www.kevingarbee.com*

RENEE GAUTHIER was born and raised in Chicago. Renee started her comedy career at the world-renowned Second City Chicago. A conservatory graduate, she continued her comedic education at Improv Olympic and The Annoyance Theater. Continuing to be a part of writing and performing with several Chicago sketch groups, Renee expanded her comedic skills by taking on stand-up comedy. After only six months, she won two stand-up competitions and was one of the first female comics to be asked to join underground comedy coalitions. A member of Second City's first-ever House Ensemble Improv team, one of three females to be a part of Chicago Underground Comedy, Renee cofounded SpitFire, the Comedy Broad Squad. Renee has been mentioned in the *Chicago Tribune* as a "stand out," in *The Chicago Reader* as "chatty and fun," and has received an editorial in the comedy section of *Time Out* magazine. Up until October 2006, Renee was a frequent performer at Zanies, Chicago and Schaumburg, IL, Improv. Now residing in Los Angeles, she has been seen on several L.A. underground stages, as well as at the famous Laugh Factory, Comedy Store, Ha Ha Comedy Cafe, and the Ontario Improv. Renee has appeared on *Last Comic Standing*, *Chelsea Lately*, *Carson Daly*, MTV, and tons more. She is now a writer and consulting producer on the MTV show *Ridiculousness*. *www.reneecomedy.com*

JESSICA GLASSBERG has written for the 13th through the 19th annual Screen Actors Guild Awards, where her jokes were featured on E!'s *The Soup*, EntertainmentWeekly.com, and Hollywood.com. For the past three years, Jessica has been the coordinating producer and writer of the holiday special, *A Hollywood Christmas Celebration at The Grove*, syndicated with EXTRA and hosted by Mario Lopez. For ten years, Jessica was the head writer of the nationally syndicated twenty-one-hour Jerry Lewis MDA Telethon, where she also performed five times. Jessica wrote and performed at the live event The Last Comic Sitting, with host Sherri Shepherd, from ABC's *The View* and featured comedian, Carol Leifer. Additionally, *The History of the Joke with Lewis Black* on the History Channel featured Jessica's comedic stylings and she has written for Disney XD's hit show, *Zeke and Luther*. Jessica has written, produced, and starred in two one-woman shows, and she currently produces and hosts a stand-up comedy showcase, *Laugh Drink Repeat*. *www.jessicaglassberg.com*

ARTHUR M. JOLLY was recognized by the Academy of Motion Picture Arts and Sciences with a Nicholl Fellowship in Screenwriting. His published plays include *A Gulag Mouse* (Finalist in 2010 Woodward/Newman Drama Award, 2010 Joining Sword and Pen winner), *Trash* (2012 Joining Sword and Pen winner), *Past Curfew*, *The Christmas Princess*, *How Blue Is My Crocodile*, *What the Well-Dressed Girl Is Wearing*, *Bath Time Is Fun Time*, *The Four Senses of Love*, *The Bricklayer*, and a collection of ten-minute plays called *Guilty Moments*. Other produced plays include *Bailing Out*, *Of Rats and Men*, *The Secret of Jarlsberg*, *Mopping the Stage*, *If You Could Go Back*, and the radio play *Thicker Than Water* (on KSUF and other NPR stations). *www.arthurjolly.com*

MOREEN LITTREL is the author of the *roman à clef*, *Lost in Manhattan*, Moreen is a comedian, a filmmaker, an actress, a writer, a photographer, a fashion editrix, and a chihuahua whisperer. In 2010, following a breakup with a Frenchman over the symbolism of a missing bedframe, she made her stand-up debut with material about a breakup with a Frenchman over the symbolism of…you get it. Two months later she was offered a contract to release her first comedy album by New Wave Entertainment, the "makers" of Dane Cook. She continues to perform in Hollywood at venues including Malo's and The World Famous Comedy Store. Since then Moreen has written, directed, and acted in two short films—*Meet the Zillas* (an absurdist comedy) and *The Hacks* (a mockumentary about comics)—and had a principal role in *House of Last Things*, a psychological suspense feature film written and directed by Michael Bartlett that is currently making the festival rounds in France, Brazil, and Germany. Originally from the south coast of Oregon, she studied creative writing and film production at the University of Southern California and Syracuse University, acting at the Beverly Hills Playhouse, improv at The Groundlings, patternmaking at the Fashion Institute of Technology, how to drive Rolls Royces, eat Beluga caviar, wear Bulgari jewelry, and flood billiard rooms at celebrity homes she managed straight out of college. After eight years in Manhattan, Moreen lives in Los Angeles for the third time, the charm. *www.moreenlittrell.com*

LAURA MANNINO is a comedian and writer living in Los Angeles. She wrote and starred in the short comedy *Ten Minute Decade* and won Best Actress in a Short Film at the 2012 Sunset Film Festival. *Ten Minute Decade* has screened at various festivals and screening series including the Big Apple Film Festival, the Beverly Hills Shorts Festival, and the New Filmmakers New York. Laura's writing has appeared on HLNTV, CNN, Say Something Funny B*tch, Comediva, College Candy, and The Higgs Weldon, The Laugh Button, Evolved World, and Funny Not Slutty Laura has performed stand-up all over New York and Los Angeles and was a first place semifinalist at the Ladies of Laughter Competition. Festival appearances include the New York International Fringe Festival, the Hollywood Fringe Festival, NYC Underground Comedy Festival, Wonder Women Week Festival, HA! Comedy Festival, Los Angeles Comedy Festival, Hollywood Comedy Festival, California Comedy Festival, and the Eagle Rock Comedy Festival. Laura received a bachelor of fine arts in drama from New York University's Tisch School of the Arts and is a graduate of Upright Citizens Brigade's improv and sketch programs. Laura performs and writes with the improv and sketch team, Potion. For more information about her, visit her website. *www.lauramannino.com*

HASALYN MODINE was the number one–rated morning newscaster in Missoula, Montana, for nearly seven years, but never being able to master "news hair," she gave it up and moved with her husband, Logan, to Los Angeles, where she's now a producer, writer, and filmmaker. Hasalyn and Logan are proud parents to five chickens and two cats— their work has screened at L.A. Comedy Festival, Lunafest, and on countless computer screens across the country. *www .aloneinaforest.com/hasalyn/*

KELLY MOLL is happily leading a double life. By day she is a corporate event planner and is required to wear a suit and respectable heels regularly. By night, she is writer with visible tattoos and an affinity for swearing and sarcasm. She is currently "nearly finished" with numerous works in progress, which range from the biographical to the highly imagined. She does her best thinking while watching the banks of the Mississippi River blaze by on the back of her husband's motorcycle. With a few more trips down the river, she hopes to knock one of the WIP's out of the park and end her tour of duty in the corporate world. She lives in Minneapolis with the aforementioned husband.

DANIELLE OZYMANDIAS That name? Yes, that's on her driver's license; no it's not the name she was born with. Half her relatives change their name at some point: her mom, her sister, her nephew... choosing your own name is a wonderful rite of passage; taking it is incredibly empowering. Danielle is a stage director. Her recent theater credits include the Hollywood Fringe Festival premiere of *The Other F Word*, and two one-acts—*Surprise* and *The Four Senses of Love* in *Random Acts: Falling in Love and other Serious Injuries* with Pacific Resident Theatre in the co-op space, where she previously directed the world premiere of *Past Curfew*. Her most notable credit is Neil LaBute's *Some Girl[s]*, the second production in Los Angeles, after the premiere at the Geffen, and the first on the West Coast to include the role of Reggie. When she's not creating theater, she does tend to write things down, and sometimes they get picked up by others, and sometimes... well, you're holding 'em in your hands, aren't ya?

KATE RUPPERT is a graduate of the prestigious New York University's Gallatin School of Individualized Study (doesn't that make sense for an individual like Kate?). She holds numerous accolades in numerous things. However, Kate hates writing about herself. We made her. And this is what she said: "Most relevant is that I drink a vodka-rocks; I'll probably have two, three, if someone else is buying. Dogs, children, parents, and black people love me. I'm never passive-aggressive. I'm funny, clearly. I lack career ambition of any kind, but I can write my way out of a paper bag, which comes in handy because most people can't form a sentence. I have very little pride, which is rare for a really funny writer, but I'm a rare breed. Speaking of rare breeds, when I'm not writing for Say Something Funny…B*tch and a blog that has something to do with a subject matter I'd rather not discuss, I have a normal-people job that affords me the exposure to some really ridiculous and endlessly dumb people. And then I write about them. Kate Ruppert lives in Queens with her hairless cat, Smalls. (I feel like bios end with sh*t like that.)"

REBEKAH TRIPP hails from the Northwest Suburbs of Chicago, where there is and can only be one baseball team: the Cubs. Since moving to L.A., Rebekah has spread her creative wings. She started her work on the L.A. stage at Antaeus theater, where she is an A2 Ensemble member and has been featured in many productions, including *The Thin Man*, *MacBeth*, and the Ovation Award–winning production of *Peace in Our Time*. Rebekah spent some time recently in Santa Barbara playing Lucrece, referred to as The Clam—not a cute nickname—in The Ensemble Theatre's production of *The Liar*. It was a lot of bum rolls, corsets, and brilliant theater. Recently Rebekah produced and acted in her own production of the Joe Orton play *Ruffian on the Stair*. While in L.A. Rebekah has taken huge advantage of the amazing improv scene, performing at I.O. West and UCB. She's put her improv skills to use in her few yet stellar TV appearances on *Girls Behaving Badly* (it was an all-girl prank show—get your mind out of the gutter) and *I Didn't Know I Was Pregnant.* You may still catch reruns of the latter TLC and Lifetime; she reenacts a woman giving birth to a baby in a toilet…of a fast-food restaurant…that she manages. It was a treat. Rebekah also loves to write and got her start on the marvelously amazing, Say Something Funny…B*tch blog. Look for more rants and raves on Rebekah's very own blog, One Hot Piece of Class. If after reading this you want even more information about Rebekah or you want to buy her a drink, check her out on her website. *www.rebekahtripp.com*

JENNY YANG was born in Taiwan and raised in Torrance, California. She is a Los Angeles–based writer and stand-up comedian whose live performances feature her signature mix of biting social commentary, sunny enthusiasm, and unflinching disregard for microphone volume. Jenny is a featured comic on Joan Rivers's 2013 Showtime documentary *Why We Laugh: Funny Women*, where she shares the joys and traumas of being a female comedian alongside such comedic heavyweights as Whoopi Goldberg, Kathy Griffin, Janeane Garofalo, Tig Notaro, Lily Tomlin, and Aisha Tyler. A top three finalist of the California's Funniest Female stand-up comedy contest, Jenny has performed at The Comedy Store, Improv Comedy Club, and The Kennedy Center for the Performing Arts in Washington, DC. Jenny is also a producer of the first-ever all-female Asian American stand-up comedy tour, Dis/orient/ed Comedy, which has successfully sold out theaters and comedy venues around Southern California, the Bay Area, and the Pacific Northwest and brought standing-room-only shows to colleges and universities throughout the country. Jenny's story and writing have been featured on the award-winning blog on Asian American issues, angryasianman.com; social media platforms for the Hulu-original pop culture series *The Morning After*; and *ISATV Weekly Rewind*, a comedic video review of the week's pop culture produced by international music superstars Far East Movement and by Wong Fu Productions, owners of one of the most-subscribed channels on YouTube. *www.jennyyang.tv*

Acknowledgments

A lot of people are awesome. Some people were more awesome in regards to this book.

They get extra thanks from Alisha Gaddis:

Thank you to Sara Camilli—best literary agent ever. You never gave up on me.

Thank you to Mary Farkas. You gave me so many ideas when I couldn't think of any by telling me stuff I said was funny. Cannibalism is back on the table.

Thank you to all the writers. You all put yourselves out there. You are my friends. Some people think you shouldn't work with your friends. I am not one of those people. It also doesn't hurt that my friends are geniuses.

Thank you to my parents. Obviously. They are the best.

And the biggest thanks of all, to my husband, Lucky Diaz. You listened to all my ideas, my rough drafts, even my rough draft's rough draft! Heck—you are the one who told me that

I am a writer, and that I should be writing (even though I disagreed). But look honey—now there is a book. You were right! And I am so thankful. Love you.